CHINESE
COOKING CLASS COOKBOOK

Fully illustrated, easy-to-follow instructions for all your favourite Chinese dishes, specially chosen by the Australian Women's Weekly food editor ELLEN SINCLAIR for easy preparation in the Australian kitchen.

Front cover: Sweet and Sour Pork, page 42. Watermelon in Ginger Wine, page 96. Back cover: Chicken and Corn Soup, page 16. Butterfly Prawns, page 36. Fried Rice, page 90. Lychees with Mandarin Ice, page 100. Cover picture by Andre Wohler. Opposite: Crab in Ginger Sauce, page 38.

Photography:
Ben Eriksson
Rodney Weidland
Andre Wohler

Produced by The Australian Women's Weekly Special Projects Division • Typeset by Photoset Computer Service Pty Ltd, Sydney, Australia • Printed by Dai Nippon Co Ltd, Tokyo, Japan • Published by Australian Consolidated Press, 54 Park Street, Sydney • Distributed by Network Distribution Company, 54 Park Street, Sydney • Distributed in UK by T.B. Clarke (UK) Ltd (0604) 23 0941.

FOR YOUR INFORMATION . . .
Most of the special ingredients used in Chinese cooking are now available at large supermarkets and food stores. You may have to visit Chinese food stores to buy such items as five spice powder, Chinese chilli sauce, and wrappers for spring rolls and wontons. You can make your own wonton wrappers, see page 108. The number of servings given in each recipe takes into account the fact that in a Chinese meal three or four dishes might be served at once.

CUP AND SPOON MEASURES
Recipes in this book use the standard metric equipment approved by the Australian Standards Association:
(a) 250 millilitre cup for measuring liquids. A litre jug (capacity 4 cups) is also available.
(b) a graduated set of four cups — measuring 1 cup, half, third and quarter cup — for measuring items such as flour, sugar, etc. When measuring in these fractional cups, level off at the brim.
(c) a graduated set of four spoons: tablespoon (20 millilitre liquid capacity); teaspoon (5 millilitre); and half and quarter teaspoons.
Note: All spoon measurements are level.

HORS D'OEUVRE

A plate of two or three different hors-d'oeuvre make a happy but light start to a Chinese meal.

Stuffed Mushrooms

YOU WILL NEED:
500g (1lb) medium-sized mushrooms
flour
salt, pepper
oil for deep-frying

STUFFING:
250g (8oz) pork mince
4 shallots
½ red pepper
1 stick celery
¼ cup finely chopped water chestnuts
2.5cm (1in) piece green ginger
1 tablespoon dry sherry
2 teaspoons soy sauce
1 egg white
1 teaspoon hoi sin sauce
¼ teaspoon salt
2 teaspoons cornflour

BATTER:
⅓ cup cornflour
⅓ cup plain flour
1 teaspoon baking powder
½ teaspoon salt
¼ cup water
¼ cup milk

1. Remove stems from mushrooms. Finely chop stems, add to prepared stuffing; mix well.

2. To make the stuffing put mince, chopped shallots, seeded and finely chopped pepper, finely chopped celery, water chestnuts, peeled and grated green ginger, sherry, soy sauce, egg white, hoi sin sauce, salt and cornflour in bowl; mix well. Fill stuffing into cavity of mushrooms. Mound the filling in the centre.

3. To make the batter, sift dry ingredients into bowl, make a well in the centre and gradually add milk and water. Mix to a smooth batter. Coat mushrooms with flour seasoned with salt and pepper. Dip in prepared batter.

4. Put mushrooms a few at a time into deep, hot oil. Fry until golden brown and cooked through, approximately five minutes. Do not have oil too hot or mushrooms will brown too quickly and not cook through. Makes approximately 20.

Spring Rolls

YOU WILL NEED:
500g (1lb) minced pork
500g (1lb) green king
prawns
1 red pepper
8 shallots
125g (4oz) mushrooms
2.5cm (1in) piece green
ginger
250g (8oz) can water
chestnuts
½ cabbage (preferably
Chinese cabbage)
3 tablespoons dry sherry
1 tablespoon soy sauce
1 teaspoon sugar
½ teaspoon salt
1 tablespoon oil
455g (14½oz) packet
spring roll wrappers
2 tablespoons cornflour
½ cup water
oil for deep-frying

NOTE: Spring roll wrappers
are available at Chinese food
stores, or make your own
from our recipe, see index.

1. Shell prawns, remove back vein, chop prawns into small pieces; chop shallots; seed and finely chop red pepper; slice mushrooms thinly, peel and grate green ginger; chop water chestnuts; shred cabbage finely.

2. Put all prepared ingredients into bowl. Add pork mince, sherry, soy sauce, sugar and salt; mix well. Heat oil in pan, cook pork mixture 3 to 4 minutes, stirring. Remove from pan, cool.

3. Put cornflour and water into bowl, mix well. Spoon tablespoonfuls of pork mixture evenly across one corner of spring roll wrapper, roll up in an envelope shape making sure edges have been brushed with cornflour mixture. Put into deep hot oil, fry until golden brown and cooked through, approximately five minutes. Makes about 25.

Ham Balls

YOU WILL NEED:
2 large chicken breasts
250g (8oz) leg ham
200g can bamboo shoots
250g can water
chestnuts
30g (1oz) dried
mushrooms
2 tablespoons dry sherry
3 teaspoons soy sauce
½ teaspoon sesame oil
1 tablespoon cornflour
3 tablespoons oil
¼ teaspoon salt
extra cornflour
oil for deep-frying

BATTER:
½ cup cornflour
½ cup plain flour
½ teaspoon salt
1 teaspoon baking
powder
¾ cup cold water
1 egg white

BATTER:
Sift dry ingredients into bowl, gradually add water, mixing to a smooth batter. Just before using batter, beat egg-white until soft peaks form. Fold into batter.

1. Cover dried mushrooms with cold water, cover bowl, stand overnight. Remove skin and bones from chicken meat. Drain bamboo shoots and water chestnuts. Very finely chop chicken, ham, bamboo shoots, water chestnuts and drained mushrooms. It is important that the ingredients are very finely chopped, or the mixture will be hard to form into balls.

2. Heat oil in wok or frying pan, add finely chopped ingredients, toss over high heat for three minutes. Add combined sherry and soy sauce, sesame oil, cornflour and salt, toss for a further two minutes. Remove pan from heat, allow mixture to cool.

3. Take tablespoonfuls of mixture, press into balls with hands, do this gently; mixture will crumble slightly if rolled too firmly. Coat balls lightly with cornflour.

4. Place a few balls into prepared batter; with spoon gently lift balls, one at a time from batter, draining slightly on sides of bowl. Place into deep hot oil, fry until golden brown; drain on absorbent paper; keep warm. Repeat with remaining balls. Makes approximately 45.

Gow Gees

YOU WILL NEED:
250g (8oz) wonton wrappers
250g (8oz) minced pork
125g (4oz) green prawns
60g (2oz) dried mushrooms
½ x 230g can bamboo shoots
6 shallots
1 teaspoon grated green ginger
1 clove garlic
2 teaspoons sesame oil
1 tablespoon soy sauce
1 tablespoon dry sherry
oil for deep-frying

SWEET SOUR SAUCE:
½ cup sugar
½ cup white vinegar
¾ cup water
2 tablespoons tomato paste
1 tablespoon tomato sauce
1 tablespoon cornflour
¼ cup water, extra

SAUCE:
Put sugar, water, vinegar, tomato paste and tomato sauce in saucepan, stir over medium heat until sugar dissolves. Mix cornflour to smooth paste with extra water, add to saucepan. Stir over medium heat until sauce boils and thickens, reduce heat, simmer one minute.

1. Using an 8cm (3in) cutter, cut wonton wrappers into circles; stack a few wrappers on top of each other and cut all at the same time.

2. Cover mushrooms with boiling water, stand 30 minutes, drain, chop mushrooms finely. Combine mushrooms with pork, shelled and finely chopped prawns, finely chopped bamboo shoots, finely chopped shallots, ginger, crushed garlic, sesame oil, soy sauce and sherry. Mix well. Place small amounts of mixture into centre of each circle.

3. Brush edges of wrappers with water, fold in half, pinch edges together firmly.

4. Drop gow gees into deep hot oil, fry until golden brown, remove, drain on absorbent paper. Don't have oil over-hot or gow gees will brown before filling is cooked. Serve with sauce for dipping.

Chicken and Banana Squares

YOU WILL NEED:
6 squares sliced bread
2 chicken breasts
2 firm bananas
2 eggs
3 tablespoons milk
flour
2 cups fresh breadcrumbs
oil for deep-frying

1. Remove crusts from bread, cut each slice into four squares. Steam or boil chicken in usual way until tender, allow to cool in water. Remove from water, remove skin from chicken. Carefully remove chicken meat from bones giving four pieces of chicken. Cut each piece of chicken in half horizontally giving eight slices of chicken; cut each slice into three. Peel bananas, cut in half horizontally, then again in half horizontally. Cut each length of banana into pieces the same size as the chicken.

2. Brush one side of each piece of bread with combined beaten egg and milk. Arrange a piece of chicken

on top of the egg glazed side. Arrange a piece of banana on top of the chicken.

3. Coat chicken-and-banana squares lightly with flour, holding chicken and banana firmly on to the bread. Dip in combined beaten egg and milk, coat well with breadcrumbs. Repeat once more with egg mixture and breadcrumbs.

4. Deep-fry in hot oil until golden brown. Drain on absorbent paper. Makes 24.

Ham and Chicken Rolls

YOU WILL NEED:
2 whole chicken breasts
4 slices ham
1 teaspoon salt
¼ teaspoon pepper
¼ teaspoon five spice powder
1 clove garlic
4 spring roll wrappers
flour
1 egg
2 tablespoons milk
oil for deep-frying

1. Remove skin from chicken breasts. Using sharp knife, carefully re-move chicken meat from bones, giving four individual pieces. Separate the fillet which runs along the bone on either side.

2. Pound breast pieces and fillet pieces out separately until very thin being careful not to tear meat. Lay fillet piece on top of each large breast, pound lightly. Spread chicken pieces with combined salt, pepper, five spice powder and crushed garlic. Roll each slice of ham and place on top of chicken, roll up firmly. Fold in ends to secure.

3. Dip chicken rolls in flour, then in combined beaten egg and milk. Place chicken roll diagonally across spring roll wrapper. Fold in ends and roll up securely. Seal end with a little of the egg mixture.

4. Deep-fry rolls in hot oil until golden brown and cooked through, about three minutes. Do not have oil too hot or rolls will brown before cooked through. Drain on absorbent paper. Cut into diagonal slices, serve with sweet and sour sauce (see index for sauce recipe).

Dim Sims

YOU WILL NEED:
500g (1lb) minced pork
250g (8oz) prawns
¼ cabbage
1 egg
2 tablespoons cornflour
6 shallots
2 teaspoons soy sauce
2 teaspoons sesame oil
½ x 250g (8oz) packet wonton wrappers
oil for deep-frying

1. Combine in bowl finely shredded cabbage, finely chopped shallots, minced pork, shelled and finely chopped prawns, egg, cornflour, soy sauce and sesame oil. Mix well. (Reserve about eight prawns, chopped, for decoration.)

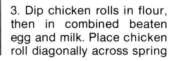

2. Place teaspoon of mixture onto centre of each wrapper.

3. Gather the sides of wrapper around filling, pleating edges together, as shown, but leaving the top open.

4. Place a small piece of reserved prawn on top of each dim sim.

5. Drop dim sims into deep hot oil, fry until golden brown. Remove, drain on absorbent paper. Makes around 50.

Hors d'oeuvre Rolls

YOU WILL NEED:
375g (12oz) pkt puff pastry
30g (1oz) butter or substitute
125g (4oz) minced pork
60g (2oz) mushrooms
6 shallots
250g (8oz) cooked prawns
1 hard-boiled egg
½ cup fine egg noodles, roughly broken
salt, pepper
1 tablespoon dry sherry
1 egg for glazing
oil for deep-frying

1. Cook noodles in boiling salted water for three minutes or until tender, rinse under hot water, drain. Heat butter in pan, add pork mince, saute until well browned. Add finely chopped mushrooms and shallots, saute further two minutes. Remove from heat, add shelled and finely chopped prawns, finely chopped egg, finely chopped noodles, sherry, salt and pepper. Mix well.

2. Cut pastry in half, roll each half into rectangle 40cm x 33cm (16 x 13in); with sharp knife trim to 38 x 30cm (15 x 12in). Cut each piece into five 8cm (3in) strips, then each strip into four 8cm (3in) squares.

3. Put a heaped teaspoonful of mixture down centre of each square. Leave edges free. Glaze edges with lightly beaten egg.

4. Roll up pastry tightly, securing edges together with beaten egg. Deep-fry in hot oil until golden. Drain on absorbent paper. Serve hot with soy sauce or sweet and sour sauce.(See index.) Makes 40.

Pork and Lettuce Rolls

YOU WILL NEED:
250g (8oz) minced pork
155g can crab
60g (2oz) dried mushrooms
6 shallots
½ x 155g can water chestnuts
½ x 250g can bamboo shoots
1 tablespoon oil
2 teaspoons sesame oil
1 tablespoon soy sauce
2 teaspoons oyster sauce
2 tablespoons dry sherry
lettuce leaves

1. Cover mushrooms with boiling water, stand 30 minutes, drain, remove stems, and chop mushrooms finely. Chop water chestnuts and bamboo shoots finely. Drain and flake crab. Chop shallots finely.

2. Heat oil in pan or wok, add pork, toss until dark golden brown. Add mushrooms, water chestnuts, bamboo shoots, crab and shallots, toss well, cook one

minute. Combine sesame oil, soy sauce, oyster sauce and sherry, add to pan, toss until well combined, remove from heat.

3. Put heaped tablespoons of pork mixture (this may vary according to the size of the lettuce cup), into the centre of each lettuce leaf.

4. Fold in the ends and sides of lettuce leaves as shown and roll up to form a neat parcel. Generally the meat filling and lettuce leaves are served separately; guests fill and roll their own lettuce leaves. Makes about 8 rolls.

SOUPS

Chinese soups come in two varieties: light and clear, thick and hearty. These are our favourites.

Mongolian Hot Pot

Mongolian Hot Pot, Chinese Steamboat — the dish has many names — which all add up to a fun way of cooking for a small party. The cooking vessel can be purchased in Chinese food stores. If you have a fondue set, this makes a good substitute. Heat the chicken stock before pouring it into the fondue pot.

The pot is set in the centre of the table, guests add their own choice of food to the simmering stock. Small strainers, shown in picture, are for lifting the food from the stock into individual small bowls.

When all the food has been eaten, the stock — which has now been transformed into a delicious soup — forms the last course.

Accompaniments set around the pot, from which guests help themselves, could be chosen from any of the following: soy sauce, chilli sauce, hoi sin sauce, sesame sauce, barbecue sauce or lemon sauce (all available in small bottles from most large supermarkets or Chinese food stores). Grated green ginger mixed with a little sugar and dry white wine, is a good accompaniment. Also have a large bowl of steamed rice.

TO PREPARE THE HOT POT:

Use heat beads available for use in barbecues. The beads must be set alight, then burnt until white hot; the best way to do this is in a barbecue or hibachi.

While the heat beads are burning, stand the hot pot on a thick piece of solid wood to protect the surface on which the pot stands.

Using tongs, quickly place the white hot beads down the chimney of the hot pot, then pour the boiling stock into the pot.

YOU WILL NEED:
250g (8oz) piece fillet steak
2 pork fillets
2 whole chicken breasts
2 large bream fillets
500g (1lb) green king prawns
240g can bamboo shoots
1 carrot
125g (4oz) bean sprouts
125g (4oz) snow peas
425g can baby corn
24 oysters in the shell or one large bottle oysters
½ Chinese cabbage
125g (4oz) bean curd
425g can straw mushrooms
185g (6oz) vermicelli

CHICKEN STOCK:
3 chicken backs (or other chicken pieces)
2½ litres (10 cups) water
3 chicken stock cubes
1 medium onion
5cm (2in) piece green ginger
1 stick celery
salt
½ teaspoon sesame oil
4 shallots

1. Prepare meat and fish. Remove all fat and sinew from steak, wrap in plastic food wrap, place in freezer for one hour or until meat is very firm. With very sharp knife or cleaver, cut meat into 3mm (⅛in) slices. Remove all fat and sinew from pork fillet, wrap in plastic food wrap, place in freezer for one hour or until meat is firm; cut as for beef fillet. Remove skin from chicken meat; cut chicken meat from each side of breast bone, giving two pieces of meat; repeat with remaining breast. Cut meat into thin slices. Remove skin and bones from fish fillets. Cut fillets into 5cm x 5mm (2in x ¼in) slices. Shell prawns, remove back vein; if large, cut in two lengthwise. Remove oysters from shell or drain bottled oysters.

2. Prepare vegetables. Wash cabbage, drain well, cut into 4cm (1½in) pieces. Cut bean curd into 5mm (¼in) slices.

Drain bamboo shoots, slice thinly. Halve mushrooms. Slice peeled carrot thinly, wash bean sprouts, top and tail snow peas, drain corn.

3. An electric hot pot (which simplifies the preparation) or a large electric frypan can be used. However, many people still have the hot pot which is fired by charcoal.

4. Make the chicken stock. Place chicken pieces, water, crumbled stock cubes, chopped celery, sliced ginger and peeled and sliced onion in pan. Bring to boil, reduce heat, simmer covered 2 hours, strain stock, return stock to pan, add salt, sesame oil and chopped shallots, bring to boil, remove from heat. To serve, bring stock to boil then pour into hot pot.

Crab Combination Soup

YOU WILL NEED:
1½ litres (6 cups) chicken stock
1 teaspoon oil
1 egg
8 shallots
30g (1oz) dried mushrooms
½ x 230g can bamboo shoots
½ teaspoon grated green ginger
155g can crab meat
125g (4oz) scallops
3 tablespoons cornflour
3 tablespoons water
2 chicken stock cubes
1 tablespoon soy sauce
1 tablespoon dry sherry
salt, pepper
2 egg whites
2 tablespoons water, extra

1. Cover mushrooms with boiling water, let stand 30 minutes. Drain, remove stalks, slice mushrooms thinly. Chop shallots, cut bamboo shoots into fine strips. Wash scallops; using sharp knife, make slit along back, and remove dark vein; slice scallops thinly. Drain and flake crab.

2. Lightly beat egg with fork. Heat oil in small frying pan, add egg, swirl egg in pan to coat sides and base of pan evenly. Loosen edges of pancake with spatula, turn and cook other side. Remove from pan, roll up, slice into thin strips.

3. Put chicken stock into large pan, bring to boil. Add mushrooms, bamboo shoots, shallots, ginger, crab meat, scallops, salt and pepper. Bring to boil, reduce heat, simmer two minutes. Remove from heat, stir in combined water, crumbled stock cubes, cornflour, soy sauce and dry sherry. Return pan to heat, stir until soup comes to boil, reduce heat, simmer uncovered for two minutes.

4. Beat egg whites and extra water lightly, add to soup in a thin stream. Stir well. Serves 6.

Long Soup

YOU WILL NEED:
250g (8oz) lean pork
8 shallots
¼ small cabbage
1 tablespoon oil
1½ litres (6 cups) chicken stock
½ teaspoon grated green ginger
2 chicken stock cubes
1½ tablespoons soy sauce
salt, pepper
125g (4oz) fine egg noodles
3 shallots, extra

1. Peel shallots, cut in thin diagonal slices. Slice pork into fine shreds. Shred cabbage finely.

2. Heat oil in large pan or wok, add pork and cabbage, fry quickly a few minutes. Stir constantly.

3. Add stock, salt, pepper, crumbled stock cubes, soy sauce and ginger. Bring slowly to the boil, reduce heat, add shallots and simmer for 10 minutes.

4. Cook noodles in boiling salted water until tender, five to six minutes; drain well. To serve, place a spoonful of noodles in soup bowls. Pour the hot soup, over, sprinkle a few extra chopped shallots on top. Serves 8.

Chicken and Corn Soup

YOU WILL NEED:
1kg (2lb) chicken
(or chicken pieces)
2 litres (8 cups) water
2.5cm (1in) piece green
ginger
1 onion
4 peppercorns
3 sprigs parsley
1 teaspoon salt
470g can creamed corn
salt, pepper
2 chicken stock cubes
1 teaspoon sesame oil
4 tablespoons cornflour
4 tablespoons water
2 egg whites
2 tablespoons water,
extra
2 slices ham
5 shallots
½ teaspoon grated green
ginger, extra
4 shallots, extra

1. The base of most Chinese soups is a good chicken stock. A whole chicken can be used. Some of the meat, when cooked, can be shredded and added to the soup, the remainder used for another meal. However, chicken pieces will serve the same purpose. You will need about 1kg (2lb) of chicken pieces. Economical chicken backs give good stock. Put chicken or chicken pieces into saucepan, add water, peppercorns, peeled and sliced ginger, peeled and quartered onion, parsley and salt. Bring to boil over medium heat, skim well to remove any scum; reduce heat and simmer gently, covered for one and a half hours. Remove any scum from top of stock, strain, reserve six cups of the stock.

2. Combine in large saucepan the reserved chicken stock, creamed corn, crumbled stock cubes, extra ginger, chopped shallots, salt, pepper, and sesame oil, bring to boil. Mix cornflour to smooth paste with the four tablespoons of water, add to soup, stir until soup boils and thickens, reduce heat, simmer one minute.

3. Beat egg whites and extra water lightly, add to soup in a thin stream, stirring well.

4. Remove meat from chicken or chicken pieces, shred finely (you'll need about one cup shredded chicken). Add thinly sliced ham and chicken meat to soup, heat gently. Top with extra chopped shallots. Serves 6.

Short Soup

YOU WILL NEED:
SOUP:
2 litres (8 cups) chicken
stock
3 shallots
½ teaspoon sesame oil
1 chicken stock cube

WONTONS:
25 wonton wrappers
(or ¼ pkt)
1 egg
water
salt

WONTON FILLING:
500g (1lb) pork mince
¼ small cabbage
1 tablespoon soy sauce
½ teaspoon sesame oil
1 teaspoon grated green
ginger

SOUP:
Finely chop shallots, add to saucepan with chicken stock, sesame oil and crumbled stock cube, bring to boil, reduce heat, simmer three minutes.

WONTON FILLING:
Combine finely shredded cabbage with pork mince, soy sauce, sesame oil and grated ginger, mix well.

1. Place a teaspoon of prepared filling slightly below centre of the wonton

wrapper. Brush around edges of wrapper with lightly beaten egg.

2. Fold wrapper diagonally in half to form a triangle. Press edges to seal, press out any air pockets around the filling.

3. Brush a dab of egg on the front right corner of each triangle and on the back of the left corner. With a twisting action, bring the two moistened surfaces together. Pinch to seal.

4. Drop the wontons into vigorously boiling salted water, cook until they float to the top, about 15 minutes; drain. Place three wontons in the bottom of each soup bowl, pour hot soup over. Serves 6 to 8.

Abalone Soup

YOU WILL NEED:
FISH STOCK:
1 large snapper head
(or 1lb fish fillets)
2½ litres (10 cups) water
2 chicken backs
2 sticks celery
2 large onions
12cm (5in) piece green
ginger
1 teaspoon salt

440g can abalone
125g (4oz) ham
1 red pepper
125g (4oz) mushrooms
2 sticks celery
2 tablespoons oil
1 teaspoon sesame oil
2 tablespoons soy sauce
salt
4 tablespoons cornflour
½ cup water
1 teaspoon sugar
60g (2oz) vermicelli
noodles

1. To make fish stock place fish, water, chicken backs, chopped celery, peeled and chopped onions, peeled and sliced ginger and salt into small boiler. Cover pan, bring to boil, reduce heat, simmer gently two hours. Allow to cool to warm, then pour stock through fine sieve. Skim off any fat on surface of stock.

2. Drain abalone; with sharp knife cut abalone into very thin slices. Finely slice ham; seed and finely slice pepper; finely slice mushrooms and celery.

3. Heat oil in large pan, add sesame oil and all prepared vegetables, saute for three minutes. Stir constantly. Add abalone, fish stock, soy sauce and sugar. Bring to boil, reduce heat, simmer, covered for 10 minutes. Season with salt.

4. Remove pan from heat. Add combined cornflour and water, stir until combined. Return pan to heat, stir until soup boils, reduce heat, simmer covered for five minutes. Break noodles in half, add to pan, simmer a further five minutes uncovered. Stir occasionally. Serves 8 to 10.

Szechuan Soup

YOU WILL NEED:
185g (6oz) lean pork
125g (4oz) ham
8 dried mushrooms
½ red pepper
30g (1oz) Chinese
pickles
½ x 225g can water
chestnuts
8 shallots
250g (8oz) prawns
1¾ litres (7 cups)
chicken stock
½ cup dry white wine
1 tablespoon soy sauce
½ teaspoon chilli sauce
½ teaspoon salt
2 tablespoons cornflour
¼ cup water
2 teaspoons vinegar
1 teaspoon sesame oil
1 egg
1 tablespoon water, extra
250g (8oz) bean curd

1. Soak mushrooms in hot water for 30 minutes; drain, squeeze dry, remove stems, slice mushrooms thinly. Cut pork, ham and pickles into fine shreds. Remove seeds from pepper, slice into thin strips. Chop shallots, slice water chestnuts. Shell prawns, remove dark vein.

2. Put chicken stock, wine, soy sauce, chilli sauce and salt into large saucepan, bring to boil, boil uncovered for five minutes. Remove pan from heat. Put water and cornflour into bowl, stir until combined. Gradually add cornflour mixture to chicken stock. Stir until combined.

3. Return pan to heat, stir until soup comes to boil, reduce heat, add ham, mushrooms, pork, pickles, water chestnuts and red pepper, stir until combined. Simmer uncovered for five minutes.

4. Stir in vinegar and sesame oil. Beat egg and extra water lightly with a fork. Gradually add to chicken stock. Stir constantly. Add shallots, bean curd cut into 1cm (½in) cubes and prawns. Simmer one minute. Serves 6.

FISH

Seafood — from crabs to prawns to whole fish — is delicious when given the Chinese touch. Try some of these recipes soon.

Barbecue Prawns

YOU WILL NEED:
500g (1lb) green king prawns
2 teaspoons cornflour
1 teaspoon salt
1 egg white
1 teaspoon curry powder
1 large onion
¼ teaspoon sugar
2 teaspoons sate sauce
3 tablespoons cream
½ red pepper
1 cup oil

1. Shell prawns. Using point of small knife, cut each prawn down the back, remove back vein; rinse, pat dry. With sharp knife, make deep slit along the back of each prawn. Put cornflour, salt and unbeaten egg white into bowl, mix well. Add prawns, mix well. Allow to stand 1 hour.

2. Heat oil in frying pan or wok, add prawns, fry quickly for 2 minutes or until prawns are just cooked; remove from pan, drain well.

3. Drain off oil from pan, leaving approximately ¼ cup oil. Add peeled and chopped onion to pan, saute 2 minutes. Add curry powder and sugar, stir for 1 minute. Add prawns to pan, stir 1 minute. Add sate sauce and cream, bring to boil, reduce heat, simmer 1 minute, stirring constantly. Add seeded and sliced pepper. Remove from heat.

4. Line serving dish with lettuce leaves, spoon prawns over. If desired, place small metal bowl in the centre of prawns. Fill bowl with warmed brandy and set alight. Pick up a prawn with chopsticks, hold over the brandy flame to heat and flavour prawns. Serves 2.

Seafood Combination

YOU WILL NEED:
250g (8oz) scallops
250g (8oz) squid
250g (8oz) green king prawns
2 large fish fillets
283g can bamboo shoots
265g can water chestnuts
8 shallots
3 sticks celery
1 teaspoon cornflour
½ cup water
1 chicken stock cube
2 teaspoons dry sherry
1 teaspoon sesame oil
2 teaspoons soy sauce
4 tablespoons oil

1. Clean scallops (see Scallop and Vegetable Combination on this page.) Now clean and prepare squid (see Squid with Broccoli in this section), shell and devein prawns, skin fish, cut into large pieces.

2. Slice celery diagonally; slice shallots diagonally; drain water chestnuts, cut in half; drain bamboo shoots, slice thinly.

3. Heat two tablespoons of the oil in pan or wok, add the prepared vegetables, saute two minutes, remove from pan.

4. Add remaining oil to pan, heat. Add scallops, squid, prawns and fish, saute two minutes. Mix cornflour with a little of the water until smooth, add remaining water, crumbled stock cube, sherry, sesame oil and soy sauce. Add sauce to wok, stir until boiling, add vegetables to wok, toss until heated through. Serves 4.

Scallop and Vegetable Combination

YOU WILL NEED:
500g (1lb) scallops
30g (1oz) dried mushrooms
2 onions
3 sticks celery
250g (8oz) beans
6 shallots
¼ cup oil
2 teaspoons grated green ginger
1 clove garlic
1 tablespoon cornflour
1 cup water
2 tablespoons dry sherry
2 chicken stock cubes
salt
1 tablespoon soy sauce
225g can baby corn

1. Using small sharp knife, make slit along dark vein of scallops. Lift out dark vein as shown in picture. Wash well, pat dry.

2. Cover dried mushrooms with hot water, let stand 15 minutes or until softened. Drain, slice thinly. Peel and quarter onions. Slice celery diagonally; string beans, slice diagonally; slice shallots diagonally.

3. Heat oil in pan or wok, add onions, celery, beans, ginger and crushed garlic, saute two minutes. Mix cornflour with a little of the water until smooth, add remaining water, dry sherry, crumbled stock cubes, salt and soy sauce. Add sauce to wok, stir until boiling. Add scallops, drained baby corn, mushrooms and shallots, cook three minutes or until scallops are tender. Serves 4.

Crispy Fish in Chilli Sauce

YOU WILL NEED:
500g (1lb) fish fillets
1 cup plain flour
⅓ cup cornflour
1 egg white
¾ cup water
oil for deep-frying

SAUCE:
1 tablespoon oil
1 tablespoon grated green ginger
3 cloves garlic
¼ cup tomato sauce
¼ cup chilli sauce
2 teaspoons sugar
1 tablespoon soy sauce
2 teaspoons dry sherry
2 tablespoons water

NOTE:
The Chinese-style chilli sauce, available from Chinese food stores, is used in this recipe.
These vary greatly in strength. The brand we used was Woh Hup.

SAUCE:
Place oil, grated green ginger, crushed garlic, the bottled tomato sauce and chilli sauce in pan. Stir over medium heat one minute, add remaining ingredients, mix well. Place chilli sauce in wok or large frying pan, add fish pieces, toss over high heat until fish pieces are coated with sauce and heated through. Serves 4.

1. Rub some salt on fingers; this makes it easier to grasp the slippery skin. Put fish skin-side down. Work from tail to head. Hold skin at tail firmly. With a sharp knife held at an angle as a lever, and using sawing motion, separate fish from skin. Remove bones from fillets, chop fish into 2.5cm (1in) cubes.

2. Sift flour and cornflour into bowl, make well in centre of sifted flours with back of spoon, add egg white and water, mix to a smooth batter, beat well.

3. Heat oil in large pan, dip fish pieces in batter to coat completely, drain off excess batter; lower fish pieces into hot oil, cook until golden brown and cooked through, about five minutes. Cooking time will depend on thickness of fish. Drain on absorbent paper.

Crisp Skin Fish

YOU WILL NEED:
2 x 500g (1lb) whole fish
oil for deep-frying
flour
6 shallots
lemon slices for garnish

BATTER:
1 cup plain flour
salt
1 tablespoon oil
1 cup water, approx.
2 egg whites

LEMON SAUCE:
2 cups water
2 chicken stock cubes
salt, pepper
5cm (2in) piece lemon rind
⅔ cup lemon juice
5cm (2in) piece green ginger
⅓ cup brown sugar, firmly packed
6 shallots
1½ tablespoons cornflour
2 extra tablespoons water

LEMON SAUCE:
Put water, crumbled stock cubes, salt, pepper, lemon rind and juice, peeled and sliced green ginger and sugar in pan. Bring to boil, reduce heat, simmer five minutes. Strain sauce, return to pan. Blend cornflour with extra water, add to sauce, stir until sauce boils and thickens; reduce heat, simmer five minutes. Stir in chopped shallots.

1. Clean and scale fish, remove dark vein from inside. Sift flour and salt into small bowl. Add oil and enough water to make a smooth batter, beat until smooth. Just before using, beat egg whites until soft peaks form, gently fold into batter.

2. Coat fish lightly with flour. Dip fish into batter to coat completely. Drain off excess batter.

3. Heat oil in large pan or wok, lower fish into hot oil. Cook until golden brown and cooked through, about 10 minutes. (If there is not enough oil to cover, turn fish once during cooking.) Drain fish well, put on heated serving dishes. Arrange lemon slices on top of fish, pour sauce over. Garnish with sliced shallots.

Prawns on Toast

YOU WILL NEED:
500g (1lb) green king prawns
1 egg
2 tablespoons cornflour
salt
pepper
thick slices of bread
1 hard boiled egg yolk
1 slice ham
1 shallot
oil for deep-frying

1. Shell prawns, leaving tails intact. Remove back vein. Cut down back, gently flatten out prawn. Combine lightly beaten egg with cornflour, salt and pepper, add prawns. Mix well to coat completely.

2. Remove crusts from bread, cut slices in half (the packaged sliced toast-bread is ideal for this.) Put one prawn, cut-side down on each piece of bread, gently flatten prawn on bread with palm of hand. With finger, rub over prawn lightly with left-over cornflour mixture (this will help topping adhere).

3. Chop egg yolk into small dice, push on to prawns near tail. Dice ham into 1cm (½in) squares, put one piece of ham in centre of each prawn. Finely chop shallot, put ¼ teaspoon chopped shallot at bottom of each prawn; there should be egg, ham, and shallot down the centre of each prawn.

4. Heat oil in large pan, gently ease Prawn Toasts into hot oil. Cook only two or three at a time. Cook until bread is golden and prawns cooked through. Drain well. Makes approximately 8.

Sate Prawns

YOU WILL NEED:
1kg (2lb) green king prawns
3 medium onions
3 tablespoons oil
1 tablespoon water

MARINADE:
¼ teaspoon five spice powder
¼ teaspoon chilli powder
2 tablespoons sate sauce
pinch salt
½ teaspoon curry powder
1 teaspoon cornflour
½ teaspoon sugar
1 teaspoon soy sauce
1 tablespoon dry sherry

1. Shell prawns; using point of small knife, cut each prawn down back and remove back vein. With sharp knife, make deep slit down back of prawn, taking care not to cut right through. Combine marinade ingredients in bowl, add prawns, mix well, stand two hours.

2. Peel onions, cut in half, then cut each half in wedges.

3. Heat oil in large pan or wok, add onions, saute until transparent, approximately two minutes.

4. Add prawns and marinade mixture to wok, saute until prawns have turned light pink and prawns are cooked, approximately three minutes; add water, mix well. Arrange lettuce leaves around edge of plate, spoon prawns over. To serve in the traditional style, place small metal bowl in centre of prawns. Fill with warmed brandy and set alight. Pick up a prawn with chopsticks, hold over brandy flame to heat and flavour prawns, as for Barbecue Prawns. Serves 4.

Crab Claws

YOU WILL NEED:
10 thick crab claws
1kg (2lb) green king prawns
6 shallots
2 sticks celery
2.5cm (1in) piece green ginger
¼ teaspoon salt
cornflour
oil for deep-frying

BATTER:
½ cup cornflour
½ cup plain flour
½ teaspoon baking powder
1 cup water
½ teaspoon salt

SWEET SOUR SAUCE:
185g can Chinese mixed pickles
1 cup water
1 teaspoon Chinese chilli sauce
2 tablespoons tomato sauce
1 teaspoon soy sauce
1 tablespoon sugar
2 teaspoons cornflour

BATTER:
Sift dry ingredients into bowl, gradually add water, mix to a smooth batter.

SAUCE:
Drain pickles, place liquid into pan. Shred pickles finely. Place pickles, water, chilli sauce, tomato sauce, soy sauce, sugar and cornflour into pan with reserved liquid, stir until combined. Stir until sauce boils. Reduce heat, simmer for three minutes.

1. The shell around the fat end of crab claws is generally lightly cracked when purchased. Gently remove the shell from fat end of claw; if necessary, tap gently with mallet or rolling pan to crack the shell further. Do not hit too heavily, or crab meat will be damaged. Leave shell on largest nipper, this makes a handle for holding the claw.

2. Shell prawns, remove back vein. Chop prawn meat very finely, until prawn meat comes together in a thick mass. Finely chop shallots, celery and peeled ginger. Place prawn meat, shallots, celery, ginger and salt into bowl; mix well.

3. Divide prawn mixture into ten equal portions. With wet hands, take one portion of prawn mixture, flatten out in palm of hand. Place meat end of crab claw into centre of prawn meat, wrap prawn meat around crab meat. Wet hands again and mould prawn meat evenly all over crab meat. Coat crab claws lightly with cornflour.

4. Holding pointed claw end of crab claw, dip into prepared batter, then place into deep hot oil, fry until golden brown and cooked through, approximately four minutes. Do not have oil too hot or batter will brown too quickly and crab claw will not cook right through. Serve one or two crab claws per person with a small bowl of prepared sweet and sour sauce. Serves 5 or 10.

Abalone in Oyster Sauce

YOU WILL NEED:
454g can abalone
30g (1oz) dried mushrooms
1 red pepper
6 shallots
½ cucumber
2 tablespoons oyster sauce
1 tablespoon white vinegar
½ teaspoon sugar
1 chicken stock cube
1 tablespoon dry sherry
2 teaspoons soy sauce
½ cup water
3 teaspoons cornflour
¼ teaspoon sesame oil
½ teaspoon grated green ginger
4 tablespoons oil

1. Drain liquid from can of abalone. With sharp knife, cut abalone into thin slices.

2. Put dried mushrooms into bowl, cover with hot water, stand 15 minutes. Drain, remove tough stalks, slice mushrooms thinly. Cut shallots into diagonal slices. Cut pepper in half, remove seeds, cut into thin strips. Peel cucumber, cut in quarters, length-wise, scoop out seeds, then cut each quarter into three or four strips.

3. Heat 2 tablespoons of oil in frying pan or wok. Add abalone and toss for one minute. Remove, keep warm.

4. Heat remaining oil in pan, add ginger, mushrooms, pepper, shallots and cucumber. Toss in pan 1 minute, add combined oyster sauce, vinegar, sugar, crumbled stock cube, dry sherry, soy sauce, water, cornflour and sesame oil. Toss mixture over high heat until sauce boils and thickens. Add abalone, allow to heat through. Serves 4.

Squid with Broccoli

YOU WILL NEED:
1kg (2lb) squid
2 onions
2 sticks celery
1kg (2lb) fresh broccoli
4 shallots
½ cup oil
2 teaspoons grated green ginger
1 tablespoon cornflour
½ cup water
2 tablespoons dry sherry
2 chicken stock cubes
3 tablespoons oyster sauce
1 tablespoon soy sauce
½ teaspoon sesame oil
½ teaspoon sugar
½ teaspoon salt

1. Hold squid firmly with one hand. With the other hand, hold head and pull gently. Head and inside of body of squid will come away in one compact piece. Remove bone which will be found at open end of squid; it looks like a long thin piece of plastic. Clean squid under cold running water, then rub off the outer skin. (Some large food stores have squid available, already cleaned, ready for cooking, as follows.)

2. Cut squid lengthwise down centre. Spread squid out flat with the inside facing upwards. With sharp knife make shallow cuts across squid in diamond shape; this helps tenderise squid and make it curl attractively when cooking.

3. Cut onions into quarters; slice celery diagonally; cut broccoli, including stalks, diagonally. Slice shallots diagonally.

4. Heat oil in pan or wok, add squid, cook until it curls, remove from pan, drain on absorbent paper. Add onions, celery, broccoli and ginger to pan, saute 3 minutes. Blend cornflour with a little of the water until smooth, add remaining water, dry sherry, crumbled stock cubes, oyster sauce, soy sauce, sesame oil, sugar and salt; mix well. Add to pan, stir until sauce boils. Return squid to pan, cook until heated through. Put on to serving dish, top with shallots. Serves 4.

Crab-stuffed Prawns

YOU WILL NEED:
1 kg (2lb) green king prawns
flour
salt
2 eggs
2 tablespoons milk
fresh white breadcrumbs
oil for deep-frying

CRAB STUFFING:
155g can crab
3 tablespoons finely chopped mixed Chinese pickles
4 shallots
1 stick celery
1 egg white
2 teaspoons cornflour
1 teaspoon dry sherry
1 teaspoon soy sauce

SATE SAUCE:
3 tablespoons oil
1 large onion
3 teaspoons curry powder
2 tablespoons sate sauce
2 teaspoons soy sauce
1 tablespoon dry sherry
1 teaspoon sugar
½ cup thickened cream

SATE SAUCE:
Heat oil in wok or frying pan, add peeled and very finely chopped onion, saute gently until onion is transparent. Add curry powder, saute for one minute. Add sate sauce, soy sauce, sherry and sugar, saute for two minutes stirring constantly. Add cream, stir until combined, bring to boil, reduce heat, simmer uncovered for two minutes or until slightly thickened. Pour sauce into four individual serving bowls, dip prawns into sauce to eat.

1. Shell prawns, leaving tail intact. Remove back vein. With sharp knife cut deeply along back of prawns, but do not cut right through. Gently pound prawns out flat with small meat mallet or rolling pin.

2. Drain crab, remove any fibrous tissue. Chop shallots and celery very finely. Place crab, Chinese pickles, shallots, celery, egg white, cornflour, sherry and soy sauce into bowl. Mix well.

3. With small spatula press approximately one tablespoon of crab filling onto flattened-out prawn. Repeat with remaining prawns and crab mixture. Gently coat prawns with flour seasoned with salt. Make sure that you keep prawns crab-side up; this is important as filling could fall off prawns. With two forks, coat prawns with combined beaten eggs and milk, then press breadcrumbs firmly on to prawns. Place in single layer on to tray, refrigerate until ready to deep-fry. Place into deep hot oil, fry until golden brown and cooked through, approximately two minutes. Do not have oil too hot or prawns will brown too quickly and not cook through. Drain on absorbent paper. Serve with prepared Sate Sauce. Serves 4.

Bamboo Prawns

YOU WILL NEED:
500g (1lb) green king prawns
3 tablespoons oil
1 teaspoon grated green ginger
1 bamboo shoot
1 stick celery
4 shallots
3 slices ham
½ cup water
1 chicken stock cube
1 teaspoon cornflour
2 teaspoons dry sherry

1. Shell prawns, make shallow cut along back of prawn and remove back vein.

2. Cut bamboo shoot into 1cm (½in) slices, then cut each slice into 5mm (¼in) strips. Cut celery, shallots and ham into strips approximately the same size.

3. Cut a 1cm (½in) slit right through prawns, along the line of the vein. Push a strip of bamboo shoot, celery, shallot and ham through slit in prawn.

4. Heat oil in wok or large frying pan, saute ginger one minute, add prawns, saute until light pink. Combine water, crumbled stock cube, cornflour and sherry, add to pan, stir until sauce boils and thickens, reduce heat, simmer one minute. Serves 4 as an entree.

Rice with Crab

YOU WILL NEED:
155g can crab meat
1 onion
6 shallots
2 tablespoons oil
2 eggs
1½ cups long-grain rice
salt
1 tablespoon soy sauce

1. Put large saucepan of water on to boil, add two teaspoons salt. When at full rolling boil, add rice gradually, so that water does not go off the boil. Boil rapidly, uncovered 12 minutes or until tender; drain well. Spread rice evenly over large shallow tray, refrigerate until cold.

2. Peel and grate onion; drain and flake crab meat.

3. Heat oil in large frying pan or wok, add onion, cook until softened. Beat eggs, pour into pan on top of onion, stir lightly, cook until set. Remove from pan, cut omelet into large strips.

4. Add rice and salt to pan, mix well. Turn rice over and over with spatula. Add crab and chopped shallots, continue cooking one minute. Add egg strips. Sprinkle soy sauce over, mix lightly; cook another minute. Serves 4.

Chinese Bream

YOU WILL NEED:
2 x 500g (1lb) bream
water
salt
2.5cm (1in) piece green ginger
3 tablespoons soy sauce
6 shallots
5cm (2in) piece green ginger, extra
3 tablespoons oil

1. Clean and scale fish, remove back vein inside fish. Two-thirds fill shallow pan with water. Add salt and crushed ginger; bring to boil, five minutes. Reduce heat, put fish in water, cover, cook 10 minutes, or until cooked.

2. Remove fish. Drain well, put on heated serving plates. While fish cooks, peel extra ginger, cut in thin slices, then into thin strips. Peel shallots, cut in thin diagonal slices.

3. Pour soy sauce over fish, sprinkle with ginger and shallots. Heat oil until nearly boiling, pour over fish. Serves 2.

Prawn Omelets

YOU WILL NEED:
8 eggs
salt, pepper
oil
60g (2oz) mushrooms
4 shallots
1 stick celery
250g (8oz) prawns
250g (8oz) can bean sprouts

SAUCE:
1 cup water
1 tablespoon cornflour
2 chicken stock cubes
1 teaspoon sugar
2 teaspoons soy sauce
salt

SAUCE:
Blend water and cornflour until smooth, add crumbled stock cubes, sugar, soy sauce and salt. Stir until sauce boils and thickens.

1. Put eggs in bowl. Season with salt and pepper. Beat with rotary beater, only until eggs are slightly frothy.

2. Heat small amount of oil in pan. Gently saute finely chopped mushrooms one minute. Remove from pan, drain, add to beaten eggs. Add finely chopped shallots,

finely chopped celery, shelled and chopped prawns and well-drained bean sprouts. Mix well.

3. Add enough oil to medium-sized frypan just to cover base. When oil is hot, pour omelet mixture into pan using cup to make four small omelets.

4. When mixture is firm on one side, separate omelets with spatula or egg-slice. Turn, cook other side. Stack on warm plate while cooking remainder of omelets; keep warm. To serve, stack two omelets one on top of the other. Spoon sauce over. Serves 4.

Butterfly Prawns

YOU WILL NEED:
750g (1½lb) green king prawns
3 egg-yolks
1½ teaspoons cornflour
salt, pepper
2 rashers bacon
oil for deep-frying

1. Shell prawns. Leave tail intact. Using point of small knife, cut each prawn down the back, remove back vein; rinse, pat dry. With sharp knife, make deep slit down back of each prawn, taking care not to cut right through.

2. Press cut side gently with fingers to flatten.

3. Beat egg-yolks and cornflour together; season with salt and pepper. Dip prawn into egg-yolk mixture. Cut bacon into 5cm x 1.25cm (2in x ½in) strips. Place strip of bacon on cut side of prawns.

4. Heat oil in wok or large saucepan. Fry prawns, a few at a time, until golden. Serves 4 as an entree.

Crab in Ginger Sauce

YOU WILL NEED:
2 crabs
3 tablespoons oil
10cm (4in) piece green ginger
1 small red pepper
8 shallots
½ cup water
2 tablespoons dry sherry
½ teaspoon sesame oil
2 teaspoons soy sauce
1 chicken stock cube
1 teaspoon sugar
2 teaspoons cornflour
¼ cup water, extra

1. Wash crabs. Gently pull away round hard shell at top.

2. With small sharp knife gently cut away the grey fibrous tissue. Rinse again to clean crab.

3. Chop off claws and big nippers. Crack these lightly with back of cleaver to break through the hard shell. This makes it easier to eat the crab meat. Chop

down centre of crab to separate body into two halves. Then chop across each half three times; this gives six body sections of crab.

4. Remove seeds from red pepper, cut into very thin strips. Chop shallots into 2.5cm (1in) lengths. Peel ginger, cut into very thin slices, then cut each slice of ginger into very thin strips.

5. Heat oil and sesame oil in wok or pan, add prepared ginger, saute very gently for two minutes, add prepared crab, toss one minute. Add red pepper, water, sherry, soy sauce, crumbled stock cube and sugar, bring to boil, reduce heat, simmer covered for four minutes, remove lid. Add combined extra water and cornflour, toss for two minutes or until sauce is boiling and coats crab well. Add shallots, toss for one minute. Serves 6.

Braised Prawns with Vegetables

YOU WILL NEED:
500g (1lb) green king prawns
250g (8oz) can bamboo shoots
250g (8oz) broccoli
470g (15oz) can straw mushrooms
1 tablespoon oil
½ cup chicken stock
1 teaspoon cornflour
1 teaspoon oyster sauce
salt, pepper
pinch sugar
½ teaspoon grated green ginger

NOTE: If straw mushrooms are not available, replace them with canned champignons (small whole mushrooms)

1. Shell prawns, using sharp knife, cut down back, remove back vein.

2. Cut broccoli into thick pieces. Drain mushrooms. Drain bamboo shoots, cut into thin slices.

3. Heat oil in pan or wok, add prawns, saute quickly until tender and light pink in colour, approximately three minutes.

4. Add to pan the bamboo shoots, broccoli and mushrooms, toss well. Blend cornflour with chicken stock, oyster sauce, salt, pepper, sugar and ginger. Bring to boil. Stir continuously and cook one minute. Serves 4.

PORK

Sweet and Sour Pork is undoubtedly one of the most colourful of all Chinese dishes. But the Chinese have other clever but so simple ways with pork.

Garlic Pork Rashers

YOU WILL NEED:
750g (1½lb) pork rashers
2 tablespoons oil
1 tablespoon canned black beans
1 cup water
2 teaspoons soy sauce
2 teaspoons grated green ginger
2 cloves garlic
2 teaspoons cornflour
2 tablespoons water, extra
2 teaspoons sherry

3. Soak washed black beans in a tablespoon of the water for 10 minutes, place in blender with remaining water, blend on high speed one minute, or mash beans well with the water. Combine soy sauce, ginger and crushed garlic, stir in black bean mixture. Place sauted rashers in pan, pour sauce over, bring to boil, reduce heat, simmer covered, one hour.

1. Chop rashers into 5cm (2in) pieces with sharp knife or cleaver.

2. Saute pork pieces in hot oil until golden brown.

4. Combine cornflour, extra water and sherry, stir until smooth. Add to pan, stir until sauce boils and thickens, reduce heat, simmer one minute. Serves 4.

Sweet and Sour Pork

YOU WILL NEED:
1.25kg (2½lb) lean pork chops
2 teaspoons sugar
3 tablespoons soy sauce
1 tablespoon dry sherry
1 egg yolk
cornflour
oil for deep-frying
1 large onion
8 shallots
1 red pepper
125g (4oz) mushrooms
1 medium cucumber
2 sticks celery
3 tablespoons oil, extra
470g (15oz) can pineapple pieces
2 tablespoons tomato sauce
¼ cup white vinegar
1 cup water
1 chicken stock cube
1½ tablespoons cornflour, extra

1. Combine sugar, 1½ tablespoons soy sauce, sherry and egg yolk, stir well. Cut meat into 2.5cm (1in) cubes, place into soy sauce mixture, stir until meat is coated. Cover, leave one hour; stir occasionally.

2. Drain meat from marinade, reserve liquid. Toss meat lightly in cornflour. Heat oil, cook meat until golden brown and cooked through, about seven minutes. Do this in several batches so meat browns well; drain well.

3. Peel and slice onion; slice shallots diagonally; slice pepper thickly, remove seeds; slice mushrooms and celery, cut the cucumber into quarters, lengthwise, remove seeds, cut cucumber into slices.

4. Heat three tablespoons oil in large pan, add all the prepared vegetables, saute three minutes. Drain pineapple and add pineapple syrup to pan with marinade from meat, remaining soy sauce, tomato sauce, vinegar and crumbled stock cube. Blend extra cornflour and water, add to pan, stir until sauce boils and thickens, Add pineapple pieces, season with salt and pepper. Add pork, stir until combined. Serves 4 to 6.

Spiced Pork

YOU WILL NEED:
1.5kg (3lb) lean pork chops
½ teaspoon five spice powder
1½ tablespoons sweet sherry
1½ tablespoons cornflour
salt, pepper
2 tablespoons soy sauce
1 teaspoon finely chopped green ginger
¼ cup water
1 chicken stock cube
2 teaspoons soy sauce, extra
oil for frying

1. Trim chops, discard the fat and bones. Mix together remaining ingredients in bowl, except chicken stock cube, water and extra soy sauce; add chops, mix well. Set aside two hours. Stir occasionally.

2. Pour oil into wok or pan: oil should be 2.5cm (1in) in depth in wok. When hot, add marinated pork chops, fry quickly on both sides until golden brown and cooked through.

3. Remove pork chops from pan, cut into serving-size pieces, keep warm.

4. Combine in pan, water, crumbled stock cube and extra soy sauce, bring to boil, pour over pork. Serve with Chinese mixed pickles scattered over. Serves 4. The pickles can be bought in cans or jars from Chinese food stores, or you can make your own using our recipe, see index.

Barbecued Pork Spare Ribs

YOU WILL NEED:
1kg (2lb) pork spare ribs
4 tablespoons barbecue sauce
4 tablespoons honey
4 tablespoons brown vinegar
1 tablespoon Chinese chilli sauce
¼ teaspoon five spice powder
⅓ cup dry sherry
2 tablespoons soy sauce
1 clove garlic
2.5cm (1in) piece green ginger

1. Put pork spare ribs in large saucepan of water. Bring to boil, reduce heat, simmer covered 20 minutes, this helps remove any excess fat.

2. Combine the barbecue sauce, honey, vinegar, chilli sauce, five spice powder, dry sherry, soy sauce, crushed garlic and grated ginger; mix well. Put pork spare ribs into baking dish, pour sauce over, leave to stand one hour; turn occasionally.

3. Bake in moderately hot oven one hour, or until pork is tender, baste frequently. Serves 4 to 6.

Trotters with Ginger

YOU WILL NEED:
4 pig's trotters
250g (8oz) green ginger
1½ cups sugar
1½ cups brown vinegar
2 thin Chinese turnips

1. Ask the butcher to cut the trotters into 5cm (2in) pieces. Place trotters into large bowl, cover with cold water, allow to stand for 15 minutes. Drain, cover with fresh water, allow to stand for 15 minutes. Drain. Place trotters in large saucepan or small boiler. Cover well with cold water. Place over heat, bring to boil. Cover and boil for one minute, drain. Cover again with cold water, bring to boil. Cover, boil for one minute, drain.

2. With small sharp knife, scrape skin from ginger, cut ginger into chunky pieces, approximately 1cm (½in). Peel Chinese turnips, cut into 2.5cm (1in) lengths.

3. Return trotters to pan, add vinegar and sugar. Add prepared ginger, stir until combined. Place pan over heat, bring to boil, reduce heat, cover and simmer two hours. Stir occasionally.

4. Add prepared turnips to pan, cover, simmer for a further 60 minutes. During last 15 minutes of cooking time, remove lid, increase heat slightly. Ginger sauce should be reduced enough to coat pig's trotters in a thick glaze. Be careful, as the reduced liquid can burn on the bottom of pan. Stir occasionally during the last 15 minutes of cooking time. Serves 4.

Steamed Pork Buns

YOU WILL NEED:
DOUGH:
3 cups plain flour
1 tablespoon baking powder
60g (2oz) lard
¾ cup warm water
1 teaspoon white vinegar
½ teaspoon salt

PORK FILLING:
2.5cm (1in) piece green ginger
1 clove garlic
2 tablespoons oil
½ cup water
1 tablespoon hoi sin sauce
1 tablespoon oyster sauce
1 tablespoon soy sauce
½ teaspoon sesame oil
3 teaspoons cornflour
4 shallots
250g (8oz) Chinese barbecued pork

NOTE:
These buns are cooked in steamers, available at Chinese stores. They are available in sets of two or three racks. Cost of a two rack steamer is around $10. Chinese barbecued pork, can be bought at Chinese food stores; or you can make your own. See our recipe in this section.

1. Place peeled and grated ginger, crushed garlic and oil in frying pan, saute gently for one minute. Add hoi sin sauce, oyster sauce, soy sauce and sesame oil, simmer for two minutes, stirring constantly. Add combined water and cornflour, stir until sauce boils; reduce heat, simmer uncovered for two minutes. Add very finely chopped pork, stir until combined. Remove pan from heat, add finely chopped shallots, stir until combined. Allow pork mixture to become completely cold.

2. To make the dough sift flour, salt and baking powder into bowl. Rub in softened lard until mixture resembles fine breadcrumbs. Add combined warm water and vinegar, stir to a soft but pliable dough. Turn out on to lightly floured surface; knead lightly. Cover dough with plastic food wrap, allow to stand for 20 minutes. Knead again lightly. Cut dough into 12 equal portions. Roll each portion into a ball.

3. Take each ball of dough and roll out on floured surface to a 10cm (4in) circle. Brush edge lightly with water. Place one round of dough in palm of hand. Put one tablespoon of filling in centre of round. Press edges of dough together.

4. Take the two ends of bun, bring them up over the pinched edge and twist together firmly. Cut 12 pieces of greaseproof paper into 12cm (5in) squares. Brush one side lightly with oil. Place a bun upside down, so the smooth rounded side is uppermost, on each oiled piece of paper.

5. Choose a saucepan slightly smaller than the diameter of the steamer you are going to use. Fill saucepan about one-third full of water, bring to boil. Arrange buns on paper in single layer in steamer. If using steamer with two or three racks, fill remaining racks in same way. Place on top of first rack. Put lid on top. Steam over gently boiling water for 20 minutes. There is no need to change position of racks during cooking time. Makes 12 buns.

Pork Ribs with Chilli Plum Sauce

YOU WILL NEED:
750g (1½lb) pork ribs
1 tablespoon oyster sauce
2 tablespoons dry sherry
1 tablespoon soy sauce
3 teaspoons black beans
1½ teaspoons five spice powder
½ teaspoon pepper
¼ teaspoon salt

CHILLI PLUM SAUCE:
2 teaspoons oil
1 clove garlic
½ teaspoon grated green ginger
2 shallots
170ml bottle plum sauce
½ teaspoon chilli sauce
1 chicken stock cube
⅓ cup water
2 teaspoons soy sauce
2 teaspoons cornflour

SAUCE:
Heat oil in small saucepan, add crushed garlic, ginger and chopped shallots. Cook over gentle heat for one minute. Remove from heat, add plum sauce and chilli sauce, stir until combined. Add combined water, crumbled stock cube, soy sauce and cornflour. Return pan to heat. Stir until sauce boils and thickens.

1. Using sharp knife, remove excess fat from ribs.

2. Cover black beans with water, leave 15 minutes, drain, mash with fork. In a bowl combine oyster sauce, sherry, soy sauce, black beans, five spice powder, pepper and salt.

3. Coat each rib with black bean mixture. Put under grill for 10 minutes. Turn occasionally.

4. Remove pork ribs from grill, brush on both sides with chilli plum sauce. Return pork to grill, continue to cook five to 10 minutes, or until golden brown and cooked through. Serve with remaining sauce. Serves 6.

Pork, Chicken with Black Bean Sauce

YOU WILL NEED:
3 pork fillets
2 chicken breasts
3 egg-whites
1½ tablespoons cornflour
oil for deep-frying
2 tablespoons canned black beans
1 clove garlic
5cm (2in) piece green ginger
1 teaspoon Chinese chilli sauce
1 teaspoon sesame oil
1½ tablespoons soy sauce
1 tablespoon dry sherry
1 tablespoon oyster sauce
1 teaspoon sugar
½ red pepper
2 shallots
⅔ cup water
1 chicken stock cube
2 teaspoons cornflour, extra

1. Remove skin from chicken breasts, cut meat from breast bones. Cut pork and chicken into thin strips, approximately 8cm x 1cm (3in x ½in).

2. Put egg whites and cornflour into bowl, mix well. Add chicken and pork strips, a few at a time; stir to coat meat completely.

3. Heat oil in pan or wok, deep-fry meat, a few pieces at a time, until golden brown and cooked through. Remove from pan, drain well. Repeat with remaining meat.

4. Soak black beans in water for 30 minutes, rinse, drain well. Put black beans, garlic, grated green ginger, chilli sauce, sesame oil, soy sauce, sherry, oyster sauce and sugar into blender,

blend at medium speed for 30 seconds or until smooth. Drain oil from pan, add black bean mixture, stir over gentle heat until mixture boils. Stir in combined water, the crumbled stock cubes and extra cornflour. Stir until sauce boils and thickens. Add chicken and pork, toss in pan to coat meat. Allow to heat through. Sprinkle with finely sliced shallots and seeded and finely sliced red pepper. Serves 4 to 6.

Sweet and Sour Pork Chops

YOU WILL NEED:
6 lean forequarter pork chops
⅓ cup cornflour
⅓ cup water
oil for deep-frying

SAUCE:
368g (13oz) jar Chinese pickled vegetables
1 cup water
1 tablespoon tomato sauce
1 tablespoon tomato paste
1 teaspoon sugar
2 teaspoons brown vinegar
2 teaspoons cornflour
⅓ cup water
extra salt

1. Remove rind and bones from pork chops. Cut pork into 4cm (1½in) pieces.

2. Combine cornflour and water in bowl. Mix until smooth. Add pork, mix well. Drop pork pieces, a few at a time, into deep hot oil, fry until golden brown and cooked through, about three minutes. Drain on absorbent paper. Keep warm.

3. Drain pickles from jar, reserve half a cup of the liquid. Put reserved liquid, water, tomato sauce, tomato paste, sugar, vinegar and half the vegetables in pan. Stir until sauce boils, reduce heat, simmer, uncovered for five minutes. Strain sauce, discard vegetables. Return sauce to pan. Add combined cornflour, salt and extra water. Stir until sauce boils and thickens.

4. Finely shred remaining half of pickles. Place pork on serving plate. Spoon over prepared sauce. Top with finely shredded pickles. Serves 4.

Barbecued Pork

YOU WILL NEED:
2 x 375g (12oz) lean pork fillets
¼ cup soy sauce
2 tablespoons dry red wine
1 tablespoon honey
1 tablespoon brown sugar
2 teaspoons red food colouring
1 clove garlic
½ teaspoon cinnamon
1 shallot

1. Combine soy sauce, red wine, honey, brown sugar, food colouring, crushed garlic and halved shallot in large bowl. Sprinkle cinnamon on top, add pork, marinate one hour, or cover and refrigerate overnight; turn occasionally.

2. Drain pork fillets from marinade, reserve marinade. Put pork on wire rack over baking dish.

3. Bake in moderate oven 30 minutes, turning frequently with tongs and basting frequently with marinade.

4. Remove from oven, put on board and allow to cool. Cut pork into diagonal slices to serve.

CHICKEN

With their subtle Oriental flavouring, there seems no end to the imaginative recipes the Chinese can conjure up with poultry. Experiment with some of these.

Lemon Chicken

YOU WILL NEED:
4 whole chicken breasts
½ cup cornflour
3 tablespoons water
4 egg yolks
salt, pepper
6 shallots
oil for deep-frying

LEMON SAUCE
½ cup lemon juice
2 chicken stock cubes
2 tablespoons cornflour
2 tablespoons honey
2½ tablespoons brown sugar
1 teaspoon grated green ginger
1¾ cups water

SAUCE:
Combine lemon juice, crumbled stock cubes, cornflour, honey, brown sugar, ginger and water in saucepan, stir over low heat until sauce boils and thickens.

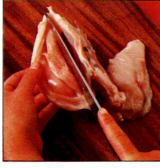

1. Carefully remove skin from chicken breasts. With sharp knife remove chicken breasts from bone, giving eight individual pieces.
2. Pound chicken breasts out lightly.

3. Put cornflour into bowl, gradually add water and lightly beaten egg yolks, add salt and pepper, mix well. Dip chicken breasts into this batter, drain well. Put a few pieces of chicken into deep hot oil, fry until lightly golden brown and cooked through. Drain on absorbent paper. Keep warm while cooking remaining chicken.

4. Slice each cooked chicken breast across into three or four pieces. Arrange on serving plate, sprinkle with chopped shallots, spoon hot sauce over. Serves 4.

Sesame Chicken Salad

YOU WILL NEED:
3 whole chicken breasts
water
½ teaspoon salt
½ teaspoon five spice
powder
2 teaspoons soy sauce
3 sticks celery
pepper
¼ teaspoon ground
ginger
1 tablespoon sesame oil
1 tablespoon soy sauce
1 tablespoon oil
1 tablespoon toasted
sesame seeds

1. To toast sesame seeds spread them on shallow tray, bake in moderate oven five minutes, or until golden brown.

2. Put chicken breasts in pan, cover with water. Add salt, five spice powder and soy sauce. Bring slowly to boil, reduce heat, simmer gently, covered, until chicken is cooked. Allow to cool in stock; drain, reserve chicken stock. Remove chicken meat from bones, cut into medium-sized slices.

3. Slice celery diagonally. Bring reserved chicken stock to boil. Add celery, boil one minute, remove celery from pan. Place in clean tea towel, squeeze gently to remove all excess moisture. Combine celery, pepper, ginger, sesame oil, soy sauce and oil, mix well. Add sliced chicken. Toss lightly. Place in serving bowl, sprinkle with toasted sesame seeds.

How to chop Chicken Chinese Style

Recipes for Chinese chicken dishes often say: "cut chicken into pieces" For Chinese dishes, chicken is cut into smaller pieces than for most other recipes. Here's the way to cut the chicken. A cleaver is good for this, or use a sharp knife.

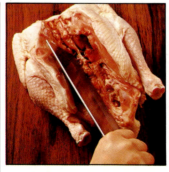

1. Stand chicken breast side up. With cleaver or sharp knife, cut right through the chicken, just a little to side of breast bone. Cut right down through back bone. Chicken is now divided into two equal pieces.

2. Cut right across both pieces of chicken. You now have two pieces each of breast-and-wing, and two of leg-and-thigh.

3. Now cut between each wing and breast (find joint, cut through this, so the piece is cut easily and cleanly). Cut or chop between each leg and thigh. You now have eight pieces.

4. Cut each chicken wing into two pieces. Chop each leg into three pieces. Chop each breast into three pieces. Chop each thigh into three pieces. You will now have 22 pieces of chicken and be ready to prepare a host of Chinese dishes.

Honey Chilli Chicken

YOU WILL NEED:
1.5kg (3lb) chicken
flour
salt
oil for deep-frying
2.5cm (1in) piece green ginger
2 tablespoons honey
2 teaspoons cornflour
⅓ cup water
1 tablespoon Chinese chilli sauce
⅓ cup lemon juice
2 teaspoons soy sauce
6 shallots

1. Cut chicken into serving-size pieces. Coat chicken pieces lightly with flour, which has been seasoned with salt.

2. Fry half the chicken in deep hot oil until golden brown. Reduce heat, cook approximately five minutes, or until chicken is cooked through. Remove from oil, drain on absorbent paper. Repeat with remaining chicken. Pour off excess oil, leaving one tablespoon of oil in pan.

3. Add peeled and grated green ginger to pan, saute gently one minute. Add honey, stir for one minute. Add combined cornflour, water, chilli sauce, lemon juice and soy sauce. Stir until sauce boils and thickens.

4. Add chicken, toss in sauce for three minutes or until chicken is heated through. Add sliced shallots, cook for a further minute. Serves 4 to 6.

Chicken with Lychees

YOU WILL NEED:
3 large chicken breasts
cornflour
425g can lychees
1 red pepper
6 shallots
3 tablespoons oil
½ cup water
2 chicken stock cubes
salt, pepper
3 tablespoons tomato sauce
1 teaspoon sugar
1 teaspoon cornflour, extra
2 teaspoons water, extra

1. Remove chicken breasts from bone, giving six individual pieces. Cut each chicken breast in half, lengthwise; cut each half into three pieces. Chop shallots into 5cm (2in) lengths. Remove seeds from pepper, cut pepper into large dice.

2. Coat chicken pieces in cornflour, shake off excess. Heat oil in pan or wok, add chicken pieces, cook until light golden brown.

3. Add pepper and shallots. Cook, stirring, one minute. Add combined water, crumbled stock cubes, tomato sauce, sugar, salt and pepper. Add drained lychees, mix well. Cover and simmer until chicken is tender, about five minutes.

4. Mix cornflour to a smooth paste with the water, add to mixture, stir until boiling. Serves 4.

Chicken Sticks

YOU WILL NEED:
1.5kg (3lb) chicken wings
¼ cup soy sauce
1 clove garlic
1 teaspoon grated green ginger
salt, pepper
1 teaspoon sugar
2 tablespoons dry sherry
2 tablespoons oil
1 tablespoon honey

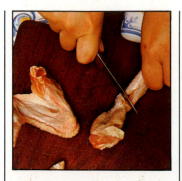

1. Wash and dry wings. Cut off wing tips at joint, as shown. (Use wing tips in another dish, or to make soup.)

2. Holding small end of bone, trim around bone with sharp knife to cut meat free from bone. Then cut, scrape and push meat down to large end.

3. Using fingers, pull skin and meat down over end of bone; they will resemble baby drumsticks.

4. In large bowl combine soy sauce, crushed garlic, ginger, salt, pepper, sugar, honey and sherry. Pour over chicken sticks, refrigerate

overnight; stir them occasionally. Pour chicken sticks and the marinade into baking dish with oil; spread them out evenly in pan. Bake in moderate oven 35 to 40 minutes or until cooked. Baste occasionally with pan juices and stir occasionally. Remove from oven, quickly brush any remaining marinade over the chicken sticks. Put on plate to serve. These make wonderful party food and are great to serve with drinks. Keep napkins handy. Makes about 24.

Marinated Chicken Wings

YOU WILL NEED:
750g (1½lb) chicken wings
6 shallots
2 cloves garlic
2 tablespoons soy sauce
2 tablespoons dry sherry
1 teaspoon grated green ginger
1½ tablespoons brown sugar
salt
3 tablespoons oil
345g (11oz) can bamboo shoots
1 tablespoon cornflour
¾ cup water
1 chicken stock cube

1. Cut shallots diagonally; put into bowl with crushed garlic, soy sauce, sherry, green ginger, brown sugar, salt and chicken wings. Mix well. Let stand one hour. Drain, reserve marinade.

2. Heat oil in wok, add drained and sliced bamboo shoots, fry two minutes. Remove from pan. Add chicken wings and shallots to pan, cook over high heat until golden brown on both sides. Reduce heat, cook further 10 to 15 minutes, or until chicken is tender.

3. Blend cornflour with a little water, add remaining water, crumbled stock cube and reserved marinade. Add to wok, stir over high heat until sauce boils, add sliced bamboo shoots, reduce heat, simmer further two minutes. Put chicken wings on serving dish, spoon sauce over. Serves 4.

Braised Duck

YOU WILL NEED:
1.75kg to 2kg
(3½lb to 4lb) duck
cornflour
2 cloves garlic
oil for deep-frying
3 teaspoons soy sauce
1½ tablespoons dry
sherry
1 teaspoon grated green
ginger
2 cups water
2 chicken stock cubes
6 dried mushrooms
230g can bamboo
shoots
225g can water
chestnuts
5 shallots
1½ tablespoons
cornflour, extra
¾ cup water, extra
½ teaspoon sugar
salt, pepper
1 teaspoon soy sauce,
extra
½ teaspoon sesame oil

The pot in which the duck is shown in final photograph can be bought at Chinese food stores and emporiums for around $9. It is an excellent vessel for braising. Before using, completely submerge the pot in cold water for 24 hours. It will break if put directly on to heat without soaking. When storing, always put about 2.5cm (1in) of water in the pot to keep it moist.

1. Wash duck, cut into serving-sized pieces. Drain water chestnuts and bamboo shoots; slice thinly. Soak mushrooms in hot water for 20 minutes. Drain, squeeze dry. Remove stalks, slice mushrooms thinly.

2. Coat duck pieces lightly in cornflour. Heat oil in pan or wok. Add crushed garlic and half the duck pieces, cook until well browned. Remove from pan, repeat with remaining pieces.

3. Drain oil from pan, add duck and combined soy sauce, sherry and ginger, cook two minutes. Stir occasionally. Add water and crumbled stock cubes, bring to boil. Put duck and liquid into saucepan, cover and simmer gently two and a quarter hours or until duck is tender.

4. Thirty minutes before cooking is completed, add mushrooms, sliced water chestnuts and bamboo shoots. When duck is tender skim off any fat, stir in combined extra cornflour, sugar, salt, pepper, extra soy sauce, extra water and sesame oil. Stir until sauce boils and thickens. Top with sliced shallots. Serves 6.

Duck with Pineapple

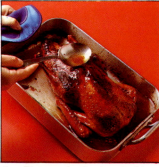

YOU WILL NEED:
1.5kg (3lb) duck
1 tablespoon oil
½ cup water
2 tablespoons bottled
barbecue sauce
2 tablespoons white
vinegar
2 tablespoons dry sherry
2 tablespoons soy sauce
¼ teaspoon five spice
powder

SAUCE:
1 small ripe pineapple
2 tablespoons oil
2.5cm (1in) piece green
ginger
1 clove garlic
¾ cup water
3 teaspoons cornflour
2 teaspoons bottled
barbecue sauce
1 tablespoon soy sauce
2 tablespoons dry sherry
1 chicken stock cube
1 tablespoon white
vinegar

1. Place duck in baking dish, pour over remaining combined ingredients. Place duck in hot oven for 20 minutes or until light golden brown, spoon marinade over frequently. Reduce the heat to moderate, cook a further 60 minutes, spoon marinade over frequently. Remove dish from oven, allow to become cold.

2. With very sharp knife or cleaver, cut duck in half. Divide each half into sections (wing, thigh, breast, leg and back). Cut these sections into small serving-sized pieces.

3. Cut top from pineapple, remove all skin. Cut pineapple into 1cm (½in) slices. Cut each slice in half then each half in three.

4. Heat oil in wok or pan, add peeled and grated ginger and crushed garlic, saute for one minute. Add duck, toss over high heat for two minutes or until duck is heated through. Add combined water, cornflour, barbecue sauce, soy sauce, sherry, crumbled stock cube and vinegar. Toss constantly until sauce is boiling. Add pineapple pieces, toss for a further two minutes or until sauce coats chicken. Serves 6.

Spiced Chicken

YOU WILL NEED:
2 x 1.5kg (3lb) chickens
1 cup soy sauce
5cm (2in) piece green ginger
2 cloves garlic
1 tablespoon five spice powder
oil for deep frying

HONEY SPICE MARINADE:
2 tablespoons honey
2 tablespoons dry sherry
½ teaspoon five spice powder
½ teaspoon sesame oil
1 tablespoon soy sauce

FRIED SALT AND PEPPER:
3 tablespoons salt
1 teaspoon five spice powder
½ teaspoon pepper

FRIED SALT AND PEPPER: Place salt and pepper into small frying pan, stir over medium heat for two minutes, add five spice powder, stir for one minute. Spoon into small individual flat bowls.

1. Fill a very large boiler three quarters full with water, add soy sauce, peeled and grated ginger, crushed garlic and five spice powder. Place lid on boiler, bring water to boil, boil for two minutes. Add whole chickens, bring back to boil, boil for one minute, then turn off heat. Allow chickens to stand in liquid, covered, until water has cooled to warm. Remove chickens from liquid, allow to drain well.

2. With very sharp, large knife or cleaver, cut chickens in half, down through centre of breast bone, then through back bone; drain any excess liquid from chickens.

3. Place chickens, cut side down, on to two trays. Make up marinade by combining all ingredients in small bowl. Rub marinade well into skin of chickens (use all marinade). Allow chickens to stand for two hours. Rub marinade occasionally into chicken skin.

4. Place one half of chicken into deep hot oil, fry until golden brown, spoon oil over chicken constantly; drain on absorbent paper; keep warm. Repeat with remaining chicken halves. When all chicken has been fried, cut into serving sized pieces with cleaver or knife. Serve with prepared fried salt and pepper for dipping. Serves 8.

Chicken with Mangoes

YOU WILL NEED:
3 whole chicken breasts
5cm (2in) piece green ginger
425g can sliced mangoes
8 shallots
¾ cup water
2 tablespoons dry sherry
1 tablespoon soy sauce
1 teaspoon sesame oil
2 tablespoons white vinegar
2 teaspoons sugar
2 chicken stock cubes
2 teaspoons cornflour
oil for deep-frying
2 tablespoons oil, extra

BATTER:
¾ cup plain flour
¼ cup self-raising flour
½ teaspoon salt
1 cup cold water

1. To make the batter sift dry ingredients into a bowl, gradually add water and mix to a smooth batter. When all the water has been added, whisk for three minutes. Cover the bowl, stand 30 minutes, whisk again just before using.

2. Remove skin from chicken breasts. With small sharp knife, gently remove chicken meat from each half of each breast, giving six pieces. Cut chicken meat into 1cm (½in) strips. Place in batter. Mix well. Remove

chicken strips one at a time from batter, drop into deep hot oil, fry until golden brown; drain on absorbent paper. Repeat with remaining chicken in batches. Set chicken aside.

3. Peel ginger, cut into wafer-thin slices. Cut peeled shallots into 1cm (½in) diagonal pieces. Cut drained mangoes into 1cm (½in) strips. Combine water, sherry, soy sauce, sesame oil, vinegar, sugar, crumbled stock cubes and cornflour.

4. Heat extra oil in pan or wok, add ginger, fry gently for two minutes, add combined soy sauce mixture. Stir until sauce is boiling, reduce heat, simmer three minutes. Add chicken, mangoes and shallots, toss for three minutes. Serve immediately.

NOTE: It is important that, once the chicken has been tossed in the sauce, it is served immediately, otherwise the batter will soften. Serves 4 to 6.

Chicken and Almonds

YOU WILL NEED:
4 chicken breasts
1 teaspoon salt
1 tablespoon cornflour
1 egg white
1½ tablespoons dry sherry
oil for deep-frying
6 shallots
125g (4oz) mushrooms
1 large carrot
½ x 230g can bamboo shoots
3 sticks celery
1 teaspoon grated green ginger
2 tablespoons oil, extra
60g (2oz) blanched almonds

SAUCE:
1 tablespoon cornflour
1½ cups water
1 tablespoon soy sauce
1 chicken stock cube
1 tablespoon dry sherry

SAUCE:
Blend cornflour with water, soy sauce, sherry and crumbled stock cube. Stir over medium heat until sauce boils and thickens.

1. Slice mushrooms roughly. Slice celery diagonally. Cut shallots into 2.5cm (1in) pieces. Slice bamboo shoots thinly, cut into 1cm (½in) strips. Peel and dice carrot.

2. Bone chicken breasts, remove skin; cut meat into 2.5cm (1in) pieces, combine with salt, cornflour, lightly beaten egg white and sherry. Mix well.

3. Deep-fry chicken pieces in hot oil until just changing colour, drain well.

4. Heat extra oil in pan, add almonds, fry until golden brown. Remove from pan, drain on absorbent paper.

5. Add grated ginger and diced carrots to pan, fry gently one minute, add remaining vegetables, saute until tender but still crisp, stirring occasionally, add chicken, heat through. Add sauce, mix through, stir in almonds. Serves 4 to 6.

Ginger-Shallot Chicken

YOU WILL NEED:
1.5kg (3lb) chicken
water
salt, pepper
5cm (2in) piece green ginger
⅓ cup oil
2 tablespoons grated green ginger extra
8 shallots

1. Wash chicken, put in saucepan, cover with water, add salt and pepper and peeled and sliced ginger. Cover, bring to boil, reduce heat, simmer gently 40 minutes, or until tender. Allow chicken to stand in water to cool.

2. Drain chicken, refrigerate until firm then cut into small serving-size pieces. It is easier to cut the chicken when it has been refrigerated.

3. Combine oil, extra ginger and finely chopped shallots in screw-top jar, season well with salt and pepper, shake to combine, refrigerate several hours. Shake again before using. To serve, spoon sauce over chicken; garnish, if desired, with extra sliced shallots. Serves 4 to 6.

Ginger-Garlic Chicken

YOU WILL NEED:
1.5kg (3lb) chicken
185g (6oz) Chinese egg noodles
cornflour
oil for frying
3 teaspoons soy sauce
1 large onion
2 tablespoons oil, extra
2 cloves garlic
2 teaspoons grated green ginger
½ cup water
1 chicken stock cube
3 teaspoons soy sauce, extra
1 teaspoon white vinegar
¼ cup tomato sauce
¼ teaspoon sugar
salt, pepper
1 teaspoon cornflour, extra
3 shallots

1. Add noodles to large quantity of boiling salted water, stir well to separate noodles. Boil uncovered three to five minutes or until noodles are tender; drain, rinse under cold water. Make sure noodles are well drained. Cut chicken into small serving-sized pieces.

2. Coat chicken pieces lightly with cornflour; shake off excess cornflour. Heat about ¼ cup oil in pan or wok. Fry a few pieces of chicken at a time until golden brown and cooked through, about five minutes. Drain well. Repeat with remaining chicken in batches. It will be necessary to discard oil and clean pan after frying one or two batches of chicken.

3. Add about another ¼ cup oil to cleaned pan or wok, add noodles and soy sauce, toss in pan until heated. Spread on serving plate; keep warm.

4. Peel onion, cut into very thin wedges. Heat extra oil in a clean pan, add crushed garlic, ginger and onion, stir fry until onion is transparent. Add chicken, mix well. Add blended water, crumbled stock cube, extra soy sauce, vinegar, tomato sauce, sugar, salt, pepper and extra cornflour. Stir fry until sauce thickens; spoon over noodles. Top with finely shredded shallots. Serves 4.

Hoi Sin Chicken

YOU WILL NEED:
1.5kg (3lb) chicken
cornflour
oil for deep-frying
3 tablespoons oil, extra
2.5cm (1in) piece green ginger
2 onions
250g (8oz) broccoli
1 red pepper
425g can straw mushrooms (or champignons)
2 tablespoons hoi sin sauce
2 tablespoons dry sherry
1 tablespoon soy sauce
2 tablespoons brown vinegar
salt
1 cup water
2 chicken stock cubes
½ teaspoon sesame oil
3 teaspoons cornflour, extra

1. Cut pepper in half, remove seeds, cut into 1cm (½in) cubes. Peel and roughly chop onions. Cut broccoli into small flowerets. Drain mushrooms; peel and grate green ginger. Cut chicken into small serving-size pieces; coat lightly with cornflour. Heat oil in frying pan or wok. Fry a few pieces of chicken at a time until golden brown and cooked through, approximately five minutes; drain well.

2. Drain off all oil from pan. Add extra oil and ginger to pan, heat gently one minute. Add onion to pan, cook over high heat for one minute. Add broccoli, pepper, and mushrooms, toss well for two minutes.

3. Add combined hoi sin sauce, sherry, soy sauce, vinegar, salt, water, crumbled stock cubes, sesame oil and extra cornflour.

4. Add chicken to vegetables and sauce, toss over high heat until sauce boils and thickens. Continue to toss for two minutes. Serves 4 to 6.

Chicken Chow Mein

YOU WILL NEED:
250g (8oz) egg noodles
2 cups oil
1.5kg (3lb) chicken
250g (8oz) lean pork
500g (1lb) green king prawns
2 medium onions
1 red pepper
2 sticks celery
¼ cabbage
8 shallots
2 teaspoons soy sauce
2 teaspoons dry sherry
1 teaspoon cornflour
4 tablespoons oil, extra
1 clove garlic
2.5cm (1in) piece green ginger
salt
½ cup water
2 teaspoons cornflour, extra
1 tablespoon soy sauce, extra
2 chicken stock cubes
1 tablespoon dry sherry, extra

1. Add noodles to large saucepan of boiling salted water, boil uncovered for four minutes, drain, rinse noodles well under hot water. Place a clean tea towel or two layers of absorbent paper on wire rack, spread noodles out on towel. Allow to stand at room temperature for three hours, or until noodles are almost dry.

2. Heat approximately two cups oil in wok or frying pan, add quarter of the noodles, fry until golden brown, turning frequently. Drain on absorbent paper. Repeat with remaining noodles in batches. Drain oil from pan.

3. Remove skin and bones from chicken, cut meat into 2.5cm (1in) cubes. Remove bones and excess fat from pork, cut meat into 2.5cm

(1in) cubes. Shell prawns, remove back vein, leaving tail intact. Peel and roughly chop onions, seed and slice pepper, slice celery diagonally, slice cabbage, chop shallots, peel and finely chop ginger. Place chicken and pork into bowl, add soy sauce, sherry and cornflour; mix well. Stand for one hour.

4. Heat extra oil in wok, add ginger and crushed garlic, saute gently for one minute. Increase heat to high, add chicken and pork, toss

constantly over heat five minutes or until meat is cooked. Add prawns, toss three minutes more. Add prepared vegetables, toss two minutes. Add combined salt, water, extra cornflour, extra soy sauce, crumbled stock cubes and extra sherry. Toss until sauce boils and thickens. Continue tossing for one minute. Place fried noodles around edge of large serving plate, spoon chicken and vegetables into the centre. Serves 6.

Beggar's Chicken

YOU WILL NEED:
1.5kg (3lb) chicken
3 shallots
2.5cm (1in) piece green ginger
1 teaspoon sugar
3 tablespoons soy sauce
2 tablespoons dry sherry
1 tablespoon water
¼ teaspoon five spice powder
2 tablespoons soy sauce, extra
2 tablespoons oil
extra oil

CLAY DOUGH:
1kg (2lb) cooking salt
4 cups plain flour
1½ cups water, approx.

NOTE:
The 1kg (2lb) cooking salt in the dough recipe is quite correct; it does not influence the taste of the chicken — just ensures that the dough bakes rock-hard as protection for the chicken during the long cooking time.

1. To make the dough place unsifted flour and salt into bowl; mix well. Gradually stir in water. Mix to a firm dough using your hands, a little extra water may be needed. Do not have dough too soft or it will be hard to handle.

2. Place two very large sheets of aluminium foil on the table, brush top sheet well with extra oil. Place the chicken in the middle of foil.

Place roughly chopped shallots, sugar, peeled and sliced ginger, soy sauce, sherry, water and five spice powder in a bowl and mix well. Rub chicken all over with extra soy sauce, then rub with the two tablespoons of oil. Rub well into the skin. Pull skin at neck end down under chicken, tuck wing tips under chicken and over neck skin. Carefully pour soy sauce mixture into chicken cavity, holding chicken up slightly so that no sauce runs out. Secure end of chicken with small skewer. Wrap aluminium foil around the chicken and secure like a parcel.

3. Roll dough out to approximately 1cm (½in) thickness, so that it will completely encase the chicken. Fold dough over the chicken. Press edges and ends together.

4. Place chicken into lightly oiled baking dish. With wet fingers, smooth out all joins, making sure there are no holes in the pastry, for the steam to escape. Bake in a hot oven for one hour. Reduce heat to moderately slow, cook further three hours. Remove chicken from oven, break open pastry clay with mallet or hammer and remove. Lift foil-wrapped chicken onto serving plate, and carefully remove the foil. Serves 4.

Chicken with Asparagus

YOU WILL NEED:
3 sticks celery
1 red pepper
6 shallots
1 teaspoon grated green ginger
297g can asparagus tips
225g can whole baby corn
2 whole chicken breasts
1 egg white
1 tablespoon cornflour
2 tablespoons oil
2 chicken stock cubes
1 tablespoon soy sauce
1 tablespoon dry sherry
2 teaspoons cornflour, extra
1½ cups oil, extra

1. Cut celery diagonally into 2.5cm (1in) pieces. Cut pepper in half, remove seeds, cut into large pieces. Slice shallots diagonally. Drain asparagus, cut in half, reserve liquid.

2. Skin chicken breasts, remove meat from bones, cut meat into 2.5cm (1in) pieces. Put chicken in bowl, combine with lightly beaten egg white, cornflour and oil,

mix well. Heat extra oil in pan or wok, add chicken pieces, fry gently until chicken is cooked through. Drain on absorbent paper. Drain excess oil from pan, leaving two tablespoons in pan.

3. Heat this reserved oil in pan, add grated ginger, celery and pepper, cook one minute.

4. Stir in chicken pieces, shallots and drained corn. Combine extra cornflour, reserved asparagus liquid, crumbled stock cubes, soy sauce and dry sherry. Pour over chicken and vegetables, stir until sauce boils; add asparagus, fold through lightly, simmer one to two minutes. Serves 4.

Combination Chop Suey

YOU WILL NEED:
2 chicken breasts
½ Chinese cabbage
125g (4oz) beans
3 sticks celery
2 onions
1 large carrot
250g (8oz) green prawns
2 tablespoons oil
250g (8oz) minced pork
1 cup water
2 teaspoons cornflour
1 chicken stock cube
1 tablespoon soy sauce
240g can bamboo shoots

3 Add cabbage, beans, carrot, onions and celery to pan, toss until all ingredients are well combined. Cook further three minutes.

1. Steam or boil chicken until tender, cool; remove meat from bones, cut into cubes. Shred cabbage; slice beans and celery diagonally; peel and chop onions; peel carrot, cut into cubes. Shell prawns, remove back vein.

2. Heat oil in pan or wok, add minced pork, cook until well browned, about five minutes.

4. Add combined water, cornflour, crumbled chicken stock cube and soy sauce to pan, stir until sauce boils and thickens. Add chicken, prawns and drained bamboo shoots, cook further three minutes, or until prawns are cooked. Serves 4 to 6.

Honeyed Chicken and Pineapple

YOU WILL NEED:
1.5kg (3lb) chicken
cornflour
oil for deep-frying
2.5cm (1in) piece green ginger
1 clove garlic
450g can pineapple pieces
1 red pepper
1½ cups water
2 teaspoons cornflour, extra
3 chicken stock cubes
1 tablespoon honey
salt
1 teaspoon sesame oil
4 shallots

1. Cut chicken Chinese-style. See how on page 54. Coat lightly with cornflour.

2. Put half the chicken pieces into deep hot oil, fry until golden brown. Reduce heat, cook approximately five minutes or until chicken is cooked through. Remove from oil, drain on absorbent paper. Repeat with remaining chicken. Pour off excess oil, leaving two tablespoons of oil in pan.

3. Add peeled and grated ginger and crushed garlic to pan, saute gently for one minute. Increase heat, add drained pineapple and seeded and thinly sliced pepper, toss quickly for two minutes. Remove from pan.

4. Add combined water and extra cornflour to pan with crumbled stock cubes, honey and sesame oil. Stir until sauce boils and thickens, season with salt. Return pineapple, red pepper and chicken to pan, toss mixture over high heat for three minutes or until chicken is heated through. Add thinly sliced shallots, toss for a further minute. Serves 4 to 6.

Chicken with Water Chestnuts

YOU WILL NEED:
1 medium onion
3 sticks celery
1 red pepper
4 dried mushrooms
225g (7oz) can water chestnuts
250g (8oz) can bean sprouts
2 whole chicken breasts
1 cup oil
⅔ cup water
1 chicken stock cube
2 teaspoons soy sauce
1 teaspoon oyster sauce
2 teaspoons dry sherry
1 teaspoon cornflour
2.5cm (1in) piece green ginger

1. Peel and quarter onion, separate layers. Slice celery diagonally into 2.5cm (1in) strips; cover mushrooms with hot water, leave 30 minutes, drain, squeeze dry; cut in half. Cut pepper in half, remove seeds, cut into 5mm (¼in) strips. Peel and thinly slice ginger. Drain water chestnuts, cut in half.

2. Skin chicken breasts, remove meat from bones, cut into 2.5cm (1in) pieces. Heat oil in pan or wok, gradually add chicken pieces, fry gently until

chicken is cooked, drain on absorbent paper. Drain oil from pan, reserve three tablespoons of oil in pan.

3. Heat reserved oil in wok, add prepared vegetables and drained bean sprouts, toss lightly, add chicken pieces, mix lightly.

4. Combine water, crumbled stock cube, soy sauce, oyster sauce, dry sherry and cornflour. Pour over chicken and vegetables, toss until sauce boils and vegetables are just tender, and still crisp. Serves 4.

Lemon and Ginger Chicken

YOU WILL NEED:
2 whole chicken breasts
3 egg whites
1½ tablespoons cornflour
oil for deep frying

SAUCE:
¼ cup lemon juice
1 cup water
2 chicken stock cubes
1 teaspoon grated green ginger
2.5cm (1in) piece green ginger
1 tablespoon cornflour
1 tablespoon water, extra
1 tablespoon honey
2 tablespoons sugar
1 shallot

1. Skin chicken breasts, remove meat from bones, cut meat into 5mm (¼in) strips.

2. Combine lightly beaten egg whites and cornflour, add chicken strips, mix well. Heat oil in wok or pan, add chicken strips, fry until golden brown. Drain on absorbent paper. Remove excess oil from pan, reserve one tablespoon. Place chicken on serving plate, keep warm.

3. Peel and thinly slice ginger. Combine lemon juice, water, crumbled stock cubes, grated ginger, honey and sugar in pan. Bring to boil. Combine cornflour and extra water, add to pan, stir until sauce boils and thickens, reduce heat, simmer two minutes. Heat reserved oil, add sliced ginger, fry one minute, add prepared sauce, simmer two minutes, pour over chicken. Garnish with chopped shallot. Serves 4.

BEEF

Beef in Chinese recipes is generally cut into very fine slices. Put the beef into the freezer for 30 minutes to make slicing easy.

Sate Beef

YOU WILL NEED:
500g (1lb) fillet steak, in one piece
1½ teaspoons soy sauce
pepper
2 teaspoons sesame oil
1 teaspoon cornflour
2 tablespoons water
2 tablespoons oil

SAUCE:
1 clove garlic
1 medium onion
3 teaspoons sate sauce
2 teaspoons dry sherry
1 teaspoon curry powder
salt
2 tablespoons water
2 teaspoons soy sauce
½ teaspoon sugar

1. Trim all fat and sinew from meat. Cut meat into 5mm (¼in) slices.

2. Gently pound each slice to flatten slightly. Put meat in bowl. Add soy sauce, pepper, sesame oil, cornflour and water, mix well. Stand 20 minutes.

3. Heat oil in wok or pan, saute meat until brown, separating each piece as it goes into the wok; brown on both sides, remove from pan.

4. Peel and roughly dice onion, add to pan with crushed garlic, saute gently until onion is transparent. Combine sate sauce, sherry, sugar, curry powder, salt, water and soy sauce. Add to onions in pan. Stir until boiling. Return beef to pan, cook until beef is tender, it should need only about a minute. Serves 4.

Beef with Noodles

YOU WILL NEED:
250g (8oz) Chinese egg
noodles
3 tablespoons oil
½ cup water
2 chicken stock cubes
salt
2 teaspoons soy sauce
500g (1lb) thick rump
steak
8 shallots
2 cloves garlic
2.5cm (1in) piece green
ginger
3 tablespoons oil, extra

1. Add noodles to large quantity of boiling salted water, boil uncovered for five minutes or until noodles are tender; drain. Rinse under cold running water and drain well. Spread noodles out on clean tea towel placed over wire rack. Allow to dry for three hours. Heat oil in wok, add noodles, toss well in oil for three minutes. Add combined water, crumbled stock cubes, salt and soy sauce. Toss over high heat for two minutes. Put onto serving plate; keep warm.

2. Remove all fat from meat, cut into 5cm x 5mm (2in x ¼in) slices.

3. Heat extra oil in wok until very hot, add meat all at once with sliced shallots, crushed garlic and peeled and thinly sliced ginger. Toss over high heat for three minutes or until well browned and cooked through. Spoon over noodles. Serves 4.

Beef with Black Bean Sauce

YOU WILL NEED:
750g (1½lb) rump steak
1 egg white
1 tablespoon dry sherry
2 tablespoons soy sauce
1 teaspoon cornflour
⅓ cup oil
4 shallots
1 red pepper
⅓ cup sliced bamboo
shoots
1 teaspoon curry powder
1 tablespoon canned
black beans
pinch sugar
⅓ cup water
2 teaspoons cornflour,
extra

3. Add two tablespoons oil to pan or wok, add shallots, red pepper, bamboo shoots and curry powder, saute two minutes, remove from wok. Heat remaining oil in wok, add meat and marinade, cook until browned.

1. Trim away any fat from steak. Cut steak into 5cm (2in) x 5mm (¼in) strips. Combine in bowl with egg white, sherry, soy sauce and cornflour, mix well. Stand 30 minutes.

2. Put beans in bowl, cover with water, stand 15 minutes, drain and rinse under cold running water. Put on to plate, add sugar and one

teaspoon water, mash well. Chop shallots into 2.5cm (1in) pieces, cut pepper in half, remove seeds, cut each half into thin strips.

4. Return vegetables to pan with bean mixture, combine well. Blend extra cornflour with remaining water, add to wok, stir until mixture boils and thickens. Serves 4.

Beef with Cashews

YOU WILL NEED:
500g (1lb) rump steak
90g (3oz) unsalted roasted cashews
8 shallots
2 cloves garlic
2.5cm (1in) piece green ginger
3 tablespoons oil
1 tablespoon cornflour
½ cup water
2 teaspoons sate sauce
1 teaspoon sesame oil
1 tablespoon soy sauce

1. Remove any excess fat from meat, cut meat into thin slices, about 5cm (2in) long. Heat two tablespoons of the oil in pan or wok, add half the beef, cook until well browned, remove from wok, brown remaining meat.

2. Chop shallots into 2.5cm (1in) pieces; peel ginger, chop finely; crush garlic.

3. Heat remaining oil in pan, add garlic, shallots, ginger and cashew nuts, saute one minute.

4. Add meat to pan with vegetables, toss well. Combine cornflour, water, sate sauce, sesame oil and soy sauce, mix well. Add to pan, stir until boiling and well combined. Serves 4.

Sherried Beef with Spinach

YOU WILL NEED:
500g (1lb) fillet steak
2 tablespoons soy sauce
2 tablespoons dry sherry
1 teaspoon sugar
½ teaspoon sesame oil
1 bunch spinach
5cm (2in) piece green ginger
2 tablespoons oil
2 tablespoons oil, extra
¼ cup water
1 chicken stock cube
½ teaspoon cornflour

1. Ask butcher to cut the eye of the fillet in one piece. Remove all fat and sinew from meat. Cut meat into 5mm (¼in) slices. Cut each slice of meat in half, then pound out gently with a mallet. Place meat into bowl with soy sauce, sherry, sugar and sesame oil; mix well. Cover bowl and refrigerate for two hours.

2. Wash spinach, shake off excess water. Cut the thick white stalks from spinach, cut these into 2.5cm (1in) slices. Cut spinach leaves into large pieces. Remove skin from ginger; cut ginger into wafer-thin slices with very sharp knife.

3. Heat oil in wok or frying pan, add white spinach stalks and ginger, saute gently for three minutes, tossing constantly; remove from pan. Heat extra oil in pan until very hot, add quarter of the meat, toss constantly for two minutes or until meat changes colour, remove from pan, repeat with remaining meat in batches. Return all meat to pan, add combined water, crumbled stock cube and cornflour, toss until mixture is boiling. Add spinach, white stalks and ginger, toss over high heat for four minutes or until spinach is wilted. Serves 4 to 6.

Ginger Beef

YOU WILL NEED:
500g (1lb) fillet steak, in one piece
2 teaspoons cornflour
2 teaspoons oil
1 teaspoon soy sauce
125g (4oz) piece green ginger
2 tablespoons white vinegar
2 teaspoons sugar
1 teaspoon salt
2 tablespoons oil, extra
1 green pepper
6 shallots
1 red chilli

1. Trim all fat and sinew from meat, slice meat into 5mm (¼in) slices. Put meat in bowl, combine with cornflour, oil and soy sauce, mix well, marinate 20 minutes. Clean, peel and thinly slice green ginger, combine with vinegar, sugar and salt in separate bowl, marinate 20 minutes or longer.

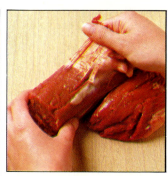

2. Heat extra oil in wok or pan, add meat slices gradually, spreading out in pan. When browned on one side, turn to brown other side; don't overlap slices or meat will not brown well. Cook quickly and only until meat is tender then remove from pan.

3. Cut pepper in half, remove seeds, chop into 2.5cm (1in) cubes.

4. Add ginger with liquid to pan with chopped pepper and shallots; cook quickly, stirring for two to three minutes. Return meat to pan, continue cooking for a further minute. Stir constantly. Serve garnished with thinly sliced chilli or sliced shallots. Serves 4.

Fillet Steak Chinese Style

YOU WILL NEED:
500g (1lb) fillet steak, in one piece
½ teaspoon bicarbonate of soda
1 teaspoon sugar
pinch salt
1 teaspoon cornflour
2 teaspoons soy sauce
1 teaspoon oyster sauce
2 teaspoons dry sherry
1 tablespoon oil
2 medium onions
1 tablespoon dry sherry, extra

1. Trim all fat and sinew from meat.

2. Slice meat into 5mm (¼in) slices. Gently flatten with meat mallet or rolling pin. Put in bowl, add soda, sugar, salt, cornflour, soy sauce, oyster sauce, and sherry. Mix well. Cover, marinate three hours.

3. Heat oil in large pan or wok. Add peeled and sliced onions and saute until just golden. Transfer to heated serving plate.

4. Add meat slices to pan gradually, spread out in pan. When browned on one side, turn to brown other side; do not let slices overlap or meat will not brown well. Cook quickly and only until meat is tender; overcooking will toughen meat. Add extra sherry, mix well. Arrange the meat over the onions. Serves 4.

Beef with Peppers

YOU WILL NEED:
500g (1lb) fillet steak
30g (1oz) dried mushrooms
2 onions
1 red pepper
1 green pepper
2 tablespoons oil
1 clove garlic
¼ teaspoon five spice powder
1 teaspoon cornflour
¼ cup water
1 chicken stock cube
1 tablespoon soy sauce

1. Soak mushrooms in hot water 20 minutes, drain, squeeze dry. Remove stems, cut mushrooms into fine strips. Remove any excess fat from meat, cut meat into thin slices. Peel and quarter onions. Seed and slice peppers.

2. Heat oil in pan, add crushed garlic, five spice powder and meat, saute until meat is golden brown. Add onions, cook further two minutes or until onions are tender but still crisp.

3. Add mushrooms and peppers, toss for two minutes.

4. Add combined cornflour, water, crumbled stock cube and soy sauce. Stir until sauce boils and thickens. Serves 4.

Beef with Celery

YOU WILL NEED:
500g (1lb) rump steak
1 teaspoon vinegar
2 teaspoons soy sauce
1 egg-white
3 tablespoons oil
6 shallots
2.5cm (1in) piece green ginger
6 sticks celery
3 teaspoons cornflour
½ cup water
1 tablespoon soy sauce, extra
1 tablespoon dry sherry
2 teaspoons oyster sauce
1 clove garlic

1. Remove excess fat from meat, cut meat into strips 2.5cm (1in) long. Combine in basin with vinegar, soy sauce and lightly beaten egg-white. Cover and stand one hour. Stir occasionally. Heat two tablespoons of the oil in pan or wok, add half the meat, brown well, remove from wok; brown remaining meat.

2. Peel ginger, chop finely, chop shallots into 2.5cm (1in) lengths, slice celery diagonally. Put celery into saucepan of boiling salted water, boil two minutes, drain, rinse under cold running water, drain well.

3. Heat remaining oil in wok, add celery, shallots, ginger and crushed garlic, saute one minute.

4. Add meat to pan, toss well. Combine cornflour with water, extra soy sauce, sherry and oyster sauce, mix well. Add to wok, stir until boiling and well combined. Serves 4.

Curried Beef

YOU WILL NEED:
500g (1lb) fillet steak
3 potatoes
2 onions
2 teaspoons curry powder
2 tablespoons oil
2 tablespoons oil, extra
3 teaspoons curry powder, extra
2 tablespoons sate sauce
1 tablespoon Chinese chilli sauce
1 tablespoon soy sauce
⅓ cup water
1 chicken stock cube
3 teaspoons cornflour
1 tablespoon dry sherry

1. Slice fillet steak thinly. Peel potatoes, cut into cubes. Peel onions, cut into quarters, separate each layer.

2. Heat oil in pan or wok, add potatoes, cook five minutes or until just tender but still crisp. Toss occasionally. Add onions and curry powder, cook further two minutes; remove from pan.

3. Heat extra oil in pan, add steak, cook until golden brown on both sides and cooked through. Add potato, onions and extra curry powder, toss for two minutes.

4. Add combined sate sauce, chilli sauce, soy sauce, water, crumbled stock cube, cornflour and sherry. Toss until sauce boils and thickens. Reduce heat, simmer three minutes. Serves 4.

Beef Chow Mein

YOU WILL NEED:
750g (1½lb) thick rump steak
2 tablespoons soy sauce
1 tablespoon chilli sauce
1 tablespoon sate sauce
1 tablespoon dry sherry
250g (8oz) egg noodles
2 tablespoons oil
125g (4oz) small mushrooms
125g (4oz) bean sprouts
1 red pepper
3 sticks celery
2 medium onions
2 tablespoons oil, extra

OYSTER SAUCE:
1 teaspoon sugar
3 teaspoons cornflour
¾ cup water
2 chicken stock cubes
2 tablespoons dry sherry
2 tablespoons oyster sauce
1 tablespoon soy sauce

1. Remove all fat from meat. Cut meat into very thin strips, approximately 5cm x 5mm (2in x ¼in) strips. Place meat into bowl, add one tablespoon soy sauce, chilli sauce, sate sauce and sherry; mix well. Allow to stand 60 minutes.

2. Peel onions, cut into wedges, separate layers of onion out. Seed pepper, cut into strips. Slice mushrooms. Slice celery.

3. Add egg noodles to large quantity of boiling salted water, boil uncovered for five minutes or until noodles are tender. Stir noodles occasionally to separate; drain well. Heat one tablespoon oil in pan or wok, add noodles and one tablespoon soy sauce, toss for two minutes, remove from pan, keep warm.

4. Heat remaining oil in pan, add onions, saute for one minute. Add remaining vegetables, toss for two

minutes, remove vegetables from pan. Heat extra oil in wok, add half the meat, fry quickly until meat just changes colour; remove from pan. Add remaining meat, work in the same way, return all meat to pan, fry. Combine all ingredients for Oyster Sauce, add to meat, toss until sauce is boiling, add vegetables, toss for a further two minutes over high heat. Place noodles on to serving plate, top with meat mixture. Serves 4 to 6.

VEGETABLES

Vegetables cooked in the Chinese manner are crisp and colourful. Because cooking time is so short, they are full of flavour.

Chinese Vegetables

YOU WILL NEED:
500g (1lb) broccoli
1 tablespoon finely chopped green ginger
2 onions
4 sticks celery
1 small bunch of mustard cabbage or spinach (approx. 6 stalks)
250g (8oz) snow peas
8 shallots
¼ cup oil
2 chicken stock cubes
¾ cup water

NOTE:
Other vegetables can be used in addition to, or in place of, those listed. Choose from thinly sliced carrots, cauliflower flowerets, sliced beans, cubed red or green peppers and sliced zucchini. Add these vegetables in step 2.

2. Heat oil in wok or large frying pan, add ginger, sliced cabbage stalks, broccoli stalks and onion; stir gently to coat all vegetables with oil, cook for one minute.

3. Add remaining vegetables, toss together lightly.

1. Prepare vegetables as shown above. Peel and quarter onions, string celery and slice diagonally, take the leaves from the stalks of the cabbage, slice the stalks diagonally, slice leaves roughly, trim stalks from broccoli, cut stalks into even diagonal lengths, (thick stalks may also be cut in half vertically); cut broccoli tops into flowerets; string snow peas; slice shallots diagonally.

4. Stir in water and crumbled stock cubes, bring to boil. Cover and cook until vegetables are just tender, about three minutes. Remove lid to stir occasionally. Garnish with sliced shallots. Serves 4.

RICE AND NOODLES

Steamed rice is an essential accompaniment to any Chinese meal, or you may prefer Fried Rice. We tell you how to cook both perfectly and also give you cooking methods for popular noodle dishes.

Fried Rice

YOU WILL NEED:
375g (12oz) long-grain rice
3 rashers bacon
250g (8oz) cooked pork
3 eggs
salt, pepper
oil
2 teaspoons grated green ginger
8 shallots
500g (1lb) prawns
2 tablespoons oil, extra
2 teaspoons soy sauce

NOTE:
A cooked pork chop, or the Chinese roast pork available from Chinese food stores, is ideal for this dish.

1. Put large saucepan of water on to boil, add two teaspoons salt. When at full rolling boil, add rice gradually, so that water does not go off the boil. Boil rapidly, uncovered, 10 to 12 minutes. When rice is tender, drain immediately. Put colander or strainer under cold running water to remove any starch still clinging to grains; drain well again.

2. Spread rice evenly over two large shallow trays, refrigerate overnight. Stir occasionally to allow rice to dry completely. If you want to serve rice the same day, spread out on shallow trays, put in moderate oven 15 to 20 minutes; stir rice every five minutes to bring the moist grains to the top.

3. Finely dice bacon, fry until crisp, drain; slice pork thinly. Beat eggs lightly with fork, season with salt and pepper. Heat a small quantity of oil in pan, pour in enough of egg mixture to make one pancake; turn; cook other side. Remove from pan, repeat with remaining egg mixture. Roll up pancakes, slice into thin strips. Finely chop shallots, shell and devein prawns, if large cut into smaller pieces. Heat extra oil in pan or wok. Saute ginger one minute, stir in rice, stir five minutes. Add bacon, pork, shallots, egg strips and prawns, mix lightly. When completely heated add soy sauce, mix well.

YOU WILL NEED:
1 packet vermicelli
oil for deep-frying

NOTE:
Vermicelli — transparent noodles — is used as a garnish, or decorative surround to many Chinese dishes.

1. Cut vermicelli bundle in half with scissors or sharp knife. Separate each half into small bunches.

2. Using tongs, carefully lower a bunch at a time into very hot, deep oil.

3. When vermicelli rises to the surface, remove immediately with tongs or slotted spoon. (The cooking time should be about four or five seconds.) Drain on absorbent paper, crush vermicelli lightly.

Noodle Baskets

YOU WILL NEED:
2 packets fine egg noodles
boiling salted water
oil for deep-frying

NOTE:
Noodle baskets are used to serve Chinese food in an unusual and attractive way. Baskets can be made several days in advance and stored, wrapped in plastic food wrap in refrigerator for three days. Or they can be wrapped and frozen; they will keep in good condition for several weeks. To reheat, place in moderately slow oven 10 minutes, until heated through. Allow longer heating time if baskets have been frozen.

1. Cook noodles in large saucepan boiling salted water until tender, five to seven minutes. Stir while boiling, to separate noodles. Pour noodles into large colander, rinse under cold running water. Drain well.

2. Place two layers of absorbent kitchen paper over wire rack. Spread noodles over, place another layer of absorbent paper over top. Stand overnight to dry.

3. Oil inside of medium-sized strainer, approximately 12cm (5in) across. Line with a layer of noodles, approximately 1cm (½in) thick. Press down well but not too firmly. Oil base of another strainer, 12cm (5in) or 10cm (4in) across. Press down lightly on to noodles in first strainer.

4. Hold handles of both strainers together. Carefully lower into very hot deep oil. Cook approximately three minutes until noodles are crisp and golden. (Cooking time depends on thickness of noodles and heat of oil). Remove from oil, carefully separate strainers, being careful not to break noodles. If necessary, run top of round-bladed knife round edge of noodles to loosen. Turn remaining strainer upside down. Carefully knock out noodle basket.

Fried Noodles

YOU WILL NEED:
250g (8oz) egg noodles
½ teaspoon salt
oil for deep-frying

1. Drop noodles into large saucepan of boiling salted water. Boil uncovered five minutes, or until tender. Separate noodles with fork as they cook.

2. Drain noodles well; spread out on oven tray which has been lined with absorbent paper; allow to dry.

3. Using tongs, drop small amounts of the noodles into deep hot oil, fry until golden brown, turning once to ensure even browning.

4. Lift noodles out of oil and drain on absorbent paper. Continue with remaining noodles in the same way. Serves 4 to 6.

Steamed Rice

YOU WILL NEED:
2 cups long grain rice
water
½ teaspoon salt

1. Put rice into strainer, wash well under cold running water. Put rice in saucepan, add sufficient cold water to come 2.5cm (1in) above rice (this applies to any quantity of rice). Add salt.

2. Bring to boil, boil rapidly uncovered until water commences to evaporate and steam holes appear in the rice. Then turn heat as low as possible, cover saucepan tightly, and allow rice to cook gently until it is tender, 15 to 20 minutes. Remove from heat, let stand for five minutes, then uncover and use as required. Serves 6.

DESSERTS

Chinese cuisine does not offer a wide range of desserts. We have included a few traditional recipes in this section, and have added some light and lovely desserts which make a superb ending to a Chinese meal.

Watermelon in Ginger Wine

YOU WILL NEED:
½ **watermelon**
1 cup water
½ **cup green ginger wine**
2 tablespoons sugar
2 pieces preserved ginger

3. Slice melon straight across, just under the scooped-out portion. Scoop out this portion of melon.

1. With rounded side of melon baller on top, press down firmly into melon.

4. Combine in pan, sugar, water and ginger wine, stir over medium heat until sugar has dissolved. Remove from heat, add finely shredded ginger, cool, pour over watermelon balls, refrigerate for several hours or overnight. Serves 4.

2. Twist melon baller around, lift out melon ball. Remove seeds, if necessary. Continue until all the top of melon has been scooped out.

Almond Junket

YOU WILL NEED:
3 teaspoons gelatine
¾ cup cold water
1¼ cups evaporated milk
½ cup sugar
¾ cup boiling water
2 drops almond essence
2 Chinese gooseberries
4 strawberries

1. Sprinkle gelatine over cold water, add sugar. Pour boiling water over, stir until sugar and gelatine have dissolved.

2. Add milk and almond essence, stir well. Pour mixture into four individual serving dishes, set aside until cool. Refrigerate until firm. Decorate with peeled, thinly sliced Chinese gooseberries and strawberries. Serves 4.

Banana Fritters

YOU WILL NEED:
2 cups self-raising flour
½ teaspoon bicarbonate of soda
1½ cups water
4 bananas
flour
oil for deep frying

1. Sift flour and bicarbonate of soda into bowl, add water, mix to a smooth batter.

2. Peel bananas, cut into three. Roll lightly in flour.

3. Drop banana pieces into batter, drain off excess batter. Deep fry in hot oil until golden brown. Remove, drain on absorbent paper. Serve hot with ice-cream. Serves 4.

Lychees and Mandarin Ice

YOU WILL NEED:
625g (20oz) can lychees
1 cup sugar
2 cups water
315g (10oz) can mandarin segments
1 tablespoon Grand Marnier
¼ cup lemon juice
315g (10oz) can mandarin segments, extra

1. Put sugar and water into pan, stir over low heat until sugar has dissolved. Bring to boil, boil uncovered for three minutes, cool.

2. Put one can of undrained mandarins in blender, blend one minute, push through sieve.

3. Add mandarin juice, lemon juice and Grand Marnier to syrup, stir until combined. Pour into tray, put in freezer until set stirring occasionally. Chill lychees and extra mandarin segments, drain and reserve syrup of lychees. Put lychees and mandarin segments into serving dishes, spoon some of the reserved syrup over. Flake Mandarin Ice with fork, spoon on top of lychees. Serves 4.

Melon with Champagne

YOU WILL NEED:
1 large honeydew melon
½ cup water
½ cup sugar
¼ cup green ginger wine
369ml bottle dry champagne
500g (1lb) sultana grapes
1 egg white
castor sugar

1. Cut melon in half. Scoop out seeds from each half. With melon baller, scoop out balls of melon, place into bowl. Cut remaining melon into pieces, reserve for another meal.

2. Place sugar, water and ginger wine into small pan, stir over low heat until sugar is dissolved. Bring to boil, boil uncovered for three minutes. Remove pan from heat, cool; place the syrup into bowl, cover and refrigerate until very cold and ready to use.

3. When buying the sultana grapes, choose small neat bunches of grapes. Cut bunches of grapes with stems large enough to hook over glasses neatly, so that grapes are held in position. With small pastry brush dipped into lightly beaten egg white, brush grapes lightly, making sure that grapes are completely covered with egg white.

4. Place grapes immediately into bowl of castor sugar, sprinkle over sugar, make sure that all grapes are coated. Place on to tray, allow to stand for two hours. Place melon balls into six individual tall glasses, place grapes at side of glasses, pour approximately one and a half tablespoons of ginger syrup into each glass, top with well chilled champagne. Serves 4 to 6.

Hot Ice-cream Balls

YOU WILL NEED:
2 litre carton vanilla
ice-cream
flour
2 eggs
¼ cup milk
packaged dry
breadcrumbs
oil for deep-frying

CARAMEL SAUCE:
60g (2oz) butter
1 cup brown sugar, firmly
packed
½ cup water
3 tablespoons Grand
Marnier or Cointreau
1 tablespoon cornflour
½ cup cream

1. It is important when making these ice-cream balls to have everything as cold as possible. Ice-cream must be very hard and should be a good quality full cream ice-cream. Put a scone tray into freezer before starting to make the ice-cream balls, so it too is very cold. Remove ice-cream container from freezer, scoop ice-cream into balls with ice-cream scoop, put on to prepared tray, return to freezer until hard.

2. Working very quickly, coat one or two ice-cream balls lightly in flour, dip in combined beaten eggs and milk, then coat firmly with breadcrumbs. Place immediately on tray in freezer; repeat with remaining ice-cream balls working as above. Freeze the ice-cream balls until very hard, then repeat egg-and-breadcrumbing to give firm coating. They can now be left for several days until you wish to serve them.

3. To fry, place ice-cream balls, two at a time, into deep hot oil, fry for 30 seconds or until golden brown, place on absorbent paper. Serve immediately with hot Caramel Sauce. Makes about 10.

CARAMEL SAUCE:
Put butter and sugar into pan, stir over heat until butter has melted, add combined remaining ingredients, stir over low heat until sugar dissolves, increase heat, bring to boil. Reduce heat, simmer three minutes, stirring constantly.

Gingered Junket

YOU WILL NEED:
2 vanilla junket tablets
1 tablespoon cold water
2 cups milk
¼ cup full cream milk powder
1 teaspoon vanilla
2 tablespoons sugar
nutmeg
preserved ginger with syrup

1. Crush junket tablets, dissolve in the cold water.

2. Put sugar and powdered milk in a bowl. Heat milk to lukewarm (do not overheat), stir into sugar and milk, add vanilla. Beat well.

3. Add dissolved junket tablets, stir in quickly. Pour into four individual serving dishes, let stand in warm place until set, about 15 minutes, then refrigerate. Before serving, sprinkle with nutmeg, arrange some sliced preserved ginger on top and spoon over a little ginger syrup. Serves 4.

Strawberry Sorbet

YOU WILL NEED:
1 punnet strawberries
1 cup water
½ cup castor sugar
2 tablespoons lemon juice
2 tablespoons Grand Marnier or Cointreau
2 egg whites
¼ cup sugar, extra

NOTE:
The sorbet can be served alone or used as a topping for fruit. We have served it over chunks of well-chilled watermelon.

1. Put water, sugar, lemon juice and Grand Marnier into blender. Add washed and hulled strawberries. Blend on medium speed for two minutes.

2. Push mixture through a fine sieve into 28cm x 18cm (11in x 7in) lamington tin. Freeze.

3. Beat egg whites until soft peaks form, add extra sugar, beat until all the sugar has dissolved.

4. Remove frozen strawberry ice from freezer, flake with a fork; fold meringue mixture through frozen strawberry mixture. Return to freezer. Freeze. Stir occasionally. Serves 4 to 6.

...AND ALL THE LOVELY EXTRAS

These pages you will find full of interest — they have all the delightful odds-and-ends that help add special interest to a Chinese meal.

Honey Walnuts

YOU WILL NEED:
250g (8oz) walnut halves
¾ cup honey
1 tablespoon lemon juice
1 teaspoon soy sauce
castor sugar

2. Drain walnuts, toss in castor sugar, coating well.

1. Combine honey, lemon juice, and soy sauce, add walnuts, mix well. Allow to stand two hours, stirring occasionally.

3. Put walnuts in enough hot oil to just cover, cook until just golden. Remove walnuts from pan, drain well. These are delicious to serve with drinks or after-dinner coffee.

China tea, one of the most thirst-quenching of all drinks, is available in many delicate and delightful flavours. Chilled, it makes a perfect iced tea, just add a slice of orange or lemon to the glass and crush it gently.

Many people prefer to blend a little China tea with a Ceylon or Indian mixture. This gives a new lightness and delicacy in taste.

TO MAKE PERFECT CHINA TEA:

China tea is taken weak, without milk or sugar. About one teaspoon of tea — or less — is used for one metric cup (250 ml, approx ½ pint) of boiling water.

China tea can be made in a teapot or in a cup. When making it in a teapot, scald the pot first with boiling water, add the measured amount of tea and at once pour in the water, which should be at a full, rolling boil. As the boiling water is added, the tea can be stirred. Cover and leave to steep for a few minutes. If you like your tea very weak add more boiling water.

When making the tea directly in the cup, rinse cup with hot water, add the tea leaves and pour on the boiling water.

When the tea is drunk, more boiling water can be poured on to the same tea leaves in the cup. Many consider this second cup the better of the two — it is lighter, even more delicate in flavour.

DIFFERENT TYPES:

China tea may be classified into the following kinds: scented, black, green, white, Oolong. Each kind comprises many varieties, each with their own special characteristics, which are further sorted and graded according to quality.

Scented tea: is manufactured from green tea, which is fully dried, then lightly scented with fragrant flowers. It possesses not only the characteristics of green tea but also the pleasant, light flower fragrance. Scented tea is named after the flower with which the tea is scented — jasmine, rosebud, orange bud or white chrysanthemum.

Black tea: is a fermented tea. During the manufacture it undergoes a chemical change, whereby the green leaves are turned red, then black after being dried thereby gaining its name.

Keemun black tea: is tightly and finely rolled and has won a wide reputation for a full, sweet taste.

Yunnan black tea: is China's high-grown black tea. It contains a large proportion of pekoe with golden tips. Fresh and strong in taste it is fragrant in aroma. (Pekoe is a grade of tea not a variety. Originally the pekoe quality was grown in Pekoe, in Southern China. Today most of it comes from Sri Lanka.)

Lapsang souchong: a special kind of black tea it is one of the most popular of all China teas and well suited to European tastes.

Green tea: is manufactured without going through the process of fermentation; the natural emerald green colour of the fresh leaves is preserved.

White tea: a kind of unfermented tea, its manufacture is different from that of green tea. It is a special product of Shui Chi, Ching Wo and Sung Chi districts in Fukien province.

Oolong tea: is a semifermented tea, fragrant in aroma, with a delicious after-taste.

These paper-thin sheets of pastry can be used as wrappers for wontons, dim sims or spring rolls. For dim sims, cut pastry to same size as shown for wontons. For spring rolls, cut pastry into 20cm (8in) squares.

YOU WILL NEED:
2 cups plain flour
1 egg
salt
¾ cup water

1. Sift flour and salt into bowl. Add beaten egg and enough of the water to mix to a stiff dough.

2. If dough is soft, add a little extra sifted flour for easier handling.

3. Roll dough out on a well-floured board until paper-thin.

4. With a sharp knife, trim edges to form 38cm x 38cm (15in x 15in) square. Trim edges. Using a ruler, cut into 8cm (3in) squares. Place squares on a tray, cover with a damp cloth until ready to use.
NOTE:
If stacking wonton wrappers for later use dust each wrapper lightly with flour before stacking.

Chocolate Ginger Lychees

YOU WILL NEED:
567g can lychees
60g (2oz) preserved ginger
185g (6oz) dark chocolate
15g (½oz) solid white vegetable shortening

1. Drain lychees, allow to stand one hour on absorbent paper, or until lychees are dry on outside. Pat occasionally with the paper to make sure they are quite dry.

2. Cut ginger into thin slivers.

3. Carefully stuff each lychee with ginger. Put chocolate and vegetable shortening in top of double saucepan. Stir over simmering water until chocolate has melted. Allow to cool slightly.

4. Dip lychees into chocolate; carefully lift out with a fork. Tap fork gently on side of saucepan to drain excess chocolate. Put on an oven tray lined with greased, greaseproof paper. Refrigerate until set. Drizzle remaining chocolate decoratively over top of each lychee. Keep refrigerated. Makes approximately 20.

Chinese Custard Tarts

YOU WILL NEED:
PASTRY:
3 cups plain flour
185g (6oz) lard
5 tablespoons hot water
pinch salt

CUSTARD:
3 eggs
⅓ cup sugar
1½ cups milk
few drops yellow food colouring

NOTE:
The yellow food colouring can be omitted from the custard, but it does give the deep coloured custard that is characteristic of these tarts.
Oven temperatures are as follows:
Electric oven:
hot 250-260C (475-500F)
moderately hot: 220-230C (425-450F)
Gas oven:
hot 200-230C (400-450F)
moderately hot: 190C (375F)

3. Roll out to 3mm (⅛in) thickness. Cut out with an 8cm (3in) fluted cutter. Put into greased patty tins.

1. To make the pastry sift flour and salt into bowl. Rub lard into flour until mixture resembles fine breadcrumbs.

2. Mix in hot water to form a firm dough. Knead lightly on lightly floured surface.

4. Beat together eggs and sugar. Gradually add milk. Mix in food colouring. Mix well. Pour custard carefully into prepared pastry cases. Bake in hot oven for 10 minutes, reduce heat to moderately hot, cook further 10 to 15 minutes, until set. Makes approx 30.

Shallot Curls

YOU WILL NEED:
1 bunch of shallots
iced water

1. Choose young fresh shallots with fairly thick bulbs. Cut bulb from shallot just where it starts to turn green, as shown in picture. (The bulbs can be used for cooking.) If shallots are long, trim green tops, leaving about 10cm (4in).

2. With sharp scissors, cut each green top down to where the hard stem starts. Make approximately eight cuts in each.

3. Put shallots in bowl of cold water with ice cubes. Refrigerate until shallots curl, approximately 30 minutes. These make an attractive garnish for Chinese food.

Gingered Cucumber

YOU WILL NEED:
2 cucumbers
1 teaspoon salt
¼ cup white vinegar
1½ tablespoons sugar
1 teaspoon grated green ginger

1. Using sharp knife, peel cucumbers, cutting as close to skin as possible. Run fork down over cut surface of cucumbers to give fluted effect when cut.

2. Cut cucumbers into thin slices. Put into bowl, sprinkle with salt; mix well. Leave to stand 30 minutes. Drain off excess liquid.

3. Combine remaining ingredients. Add to cucumber; mix well. Refrigerate several hours before serving.

Sesame Peanut Candy

YOU WILL NEED:
2 cups sugar
⅓ cup white vinegar
1 tablespoon water
½ cup toasted sesame seeds
1½ cups unsalted roasted peanuts (without red skins)

1. Combine sugar, vinegar and water in saucepan. Stir over low heat until sugar dissolves. Bring to boil; do not stir.

2. Boil mixture approximately 10 minutes or until golden brown. To test, drop a little toffee in cold water; it should form a hard ball when moulded in the water with fingers.

3. While toffee is boiling, oil a 18 x 28cm (7 x 11in) lamington tin. Sprinkle half the toasted sesame seeds and all the nuts over base of tin. Pour the hot toffee evenly over this.

4. Smooth surface over with the back of an oiled wooden spoon. Sprinkle over remaining sesame seeds, cool slightly. Cut candy into strips before it is completely cold.

NOTE:
To toast sesame seeds, spread them on shallow tray, bake in a moderate oven five minutes, or until golden.

Chinese Mixed Pickles

YOU WILL NEED:
2 carrots
1 large Chinese white radish (or 2 turnips)
1 large cucumber
1 red pepper
1 green pepper
4 sticks celery
10cm (4in) piece green ginger
8 shallots

PICKLING LIQUID:
2¼ cups sugar
2¼ cups white vinegar
1 teaspoon salt
1¼ cups water

PICKLING LIQUID:
Combine all ingredients in saucepan, stir over low heat until sugar dissolves; bring to boil. Remove from heat and cool.

1. Wash all vegetables. Peel carrots and Chinese radish, cut into thin strips. Cut cucumber lengthwise, remove seeds, cut into strips. Wash and seed peppers, cut into 2.5cm (1in) cubes. Slice celery diagonally. Peel ginger, slice thinly. Slice shallots diagonally.

2. Put large saucepan of water on to boil, bring to fast boil. Add prepared vegetables, then remove from heat immediately. Leave vegetables in water for two minutes.

3. Drain vegetables, spread on absorbent paper over wire rack for several hours to dry.

4. Pack vegetables firmly into large preserving jar or jars. Pour cold liquid carefully into jar, making sure vegetables are completely covered. Seal, store in refrigerator. Stand one week before using.

Fried Wontons

YOU WILL NEED:
½ pkt wonton wrappers
(approx 50 wrappers)
500g (1lb) lean minced
pork
1 cup finely chopped
uncooked spinach
30g (1oz) dried
mushrooms
1 tablespoon dry sherry
salt, pepper
oil for deep frying

**SWEET AND SOUR
SAUCE:**
½ cup white vinegar
1 cup canned pineapple
juice
2 teaspoons soy sauce
3 teaspoons tomato
sauce
½ cup sugar
2 tablespoons cornflour
¼ cup water
184g (6½oz) can or jar
Chinese mixed pickles

1. Put dried mushrooms in bowl, pour hot water over, stand 30 minutes, drain, squeeze dry, chop finely. Put into bowl with pork mince, spinach, sherry, salt and pepper. Mix well. Put a teaspoon of mixture in centre of each wonton wrapper.

2. Gather edges of wonton wrapper around filling, press together firmly at top, above filling.

3. Put vinegar, pineapple juice, soy sauce, tomato sauce and sugar in sauce-pan, bring to boil. Add combined cornflour and water, stir until sauce boils and thickens, reduce heat, simmer three minutes. Add drained and sliced pickles, cook further three minutes.

4. Heat oil in pan or wok, deep-fry wontons until golden brown, drain on absorbent paper. To serve, spoon hot sauce over wontons. Makes approx 50.

Bean Curd with Oyster Sauce

YOU WILL NEED:
250g (8oz) bean curd
3 sticks celery
6 shallots
1 red pepper
125g (4oz) mushrooms
3 teaspoons cornflour
½ cup water
2 tablespoons oyster
sauce
1 tablespoon soy sauce
1 tablespoon dry sherry
2 tablespoons oil

1. Cut bean curd into 2.5cm (1in) cubes, slice celery diagonally, chop shallots into 2.5cm (1in) lengths, seed pepper and cut into chunks, slice mushrooms.

2. Heat one tablespoon of the oil in pan or wok, add the bean curd, toss until lightly browned, remove from pan.

3. Heat remaining oil in pan, add celery, shallots, pepper and mushrooms, saute one minute.

4. Add bean curd to pan, toss lightly. Combine cornflour, water, oyster sauce, soy sauce and sherry. Add to pan, stir until sauce boils, toss well. Serves 4.

RESTAURANT SPECIALS

We asked some of our top restaurants to part with a favourite recipe.

Crab in Black Bean Sauce

From the New Tai Yuen Restaurant, Dixon Street, Sydney, comes one of the most popular of all Chinese dishes. The New Tai Yuen starts with green (uncooked) crabs. If you are able to obtain these, cut and clean as below, toss crab pieces in a little hot oil until they change colour, then proceed as in the recipe.

YOU WILL NEED:
2 medium crabs
3 tablespoons black beans
2.5cm (1in) piece green ginger
2 cloves garlic
3 tablespoons oil
2 tablespoons water
8 shallots
3 tablespoons oil, extra
1 chicken stock cube
¾ cup water, extra
2 teaspoons cornflour

1. Wash crabs. Gently pull away round hard shell at top.

2. With small sharp knife gently cut away the grey fibrous tissue. Rinse again to clean inside of crab.

3. Chop off claws and big nippers. Crack these lightly with back of cleaver to break through the hard shell. This makes it easier to eat the crab meat. Chop down centre of crab to separate body into two halves. Then chop across each half three times; this gives six body sections of crab.

4. Place black beans into a bowl of cold water. Mix well, allow to stand 10 minutes. Drain, rinse beans well under cold running water. Place black beans, peeled and grated ginger, crushed garlic and oil into small bowl, mash well with fork until black beans are finely crushed, add water, mix well. If you have a blender, place the ingredients plus two tablespoons of water into electric blender, blend on medium speed for 30 seconds or until roughly mashed.

5. Heat extra oil in wok or large pan, add black bean mixture, saute gently for two minutes. Stir constantly. Add prepared crab, toss for one minute. Add half a cup of the extra water and crumbled stock cube, bring to boil, reduce heat, simmer covered for four minutes. Remove lid, add combined remaining quarter cup water and cornflour, toss crab well until sauce thickens and lightly coats the crab. Add chopped shallots, toss for 30 seconds. Serves 6.

Billy Kee Chicken

This recipe is from the well-known Four Seas Restaurant in Elizabeth Street, Redfern. Billy Kee chicken is one of the most popular items on the menu.

YOU WILL NEED:
1.5kg (3lb) chicken
3 egg yolks
oil for deep-frying
½ cup tomato sauce
½ cup dry red wine
1 teaspoon worcestershire sauce
salt
pepper

1. Cut chicken into serving-sized pieces; remove skin, cut meat away from bones.

2. Chop chicken into small pieces. Add to lightly beaten egg yolks; mix well.

3. Heat oil in pan or wok, deep-fry chicken, a few pieces at a time, until lightly browned; remove from pan, drain well.

4. Drain oil from pan. Add to pan combined wine, tomato sauce and worcestershire sauce. Stir over heat until sauce boils. Add chicken pieces, mix well, allow to heat through. Season with salt and pepper. Serves 4 to 6.

Sizzling Steak

Devotees of Chinese food consider the journey to Malabar, Sydney, well worthwhile. For Malabar is the home of The Golden Lily, rapidly acquiring a reputation for some of the best Chinese food in town. This recipe comes to the table sizzling and succulent. The steak plate, with its wooden base, costs about $3 to $4 at most large department stores. Guests help themselves from the serving plate, putting the steak into individual bowls.

YOU WILL NEED:
500g (1lb) fillet steak
¼ cup water
¼ teaspoon bicarbonate of soda
3 onions
4 tablespoons oil
¼ cup worcestershire sauce
½ cup tomato sauce
½ cup sugar
1 tablespoon white wine

1. Slice meat thinly, flatten each piece with meat mallet, put into bowl. Peel onions, cut into wedges. Combine water and bicarbonate of soda, pour over steak, leave to stand one hour; drain well. This helps to tenderize the meat.

2. Heat one tablespoon oil in pan or wok, add steak, toss one to two minutes over very high heat to evaporate water; drain. Pour

off oil from pan. Heat two tablespoons oil in pan, return steak to pan, cook until well browned over high heat. Remove from pan.

3. Put cast iron steak plate in very hot oven for approximately 10 minutes or until plate is very hot. Heat remaining tablespoon of oil in pan, add peeled and quartered onions, saute quickly until golden brown and still crisp. Remove from pan, keep warm.

4. Return steak to pan, toss one minute. Add combined worcestershire and tomato sauces and sugar, stir until sauce boils, reduce heat, simmer two minutes. Remove steak plate from oven with handle, place on wooden base; arrange onions on steak plate. Spoon meat and sauce over onions. Pour wine over the steak plate immediately to give the characteristic "sizzle."

Flower Blossoms

This hors d'oeuvre comes from The Dixon Restaurant, Dixon Street, Sydney — one of Chinatown's best known and respected restaurants.

YOU WILL NEED:
PASTRY:
2 cups plain flour
salt
1 egg
¾ cup water
oil for deep-frying

FILLING:
250g (8oz) minced pork
1 small onion
3 shallots
½ x 230g can water chestnuts
60g (2oz) dried mushrooms
1 tablespoon soy sauce
1 tablespoon dry sherry
1 teaspoon grated green ginger
salt

1. To make the pastry sift flour and salt into bowl. Add beaten egg and enough water to mix to a stiff dough. Cut dough in half, roll out each half thinly to a 40cm x 25cm (16in x 10in) rectangle.

2. To make the filling cover mushrooms with boiling water, stand 30 minutes. Drain and chop finely. Combine with pork mince, peeled and finely chopped

onion, chopped shallots, finely chopped water chestnuts, soy sauce, sherry, ginger and salt. Form half the mixture in a log down one side of pastry.

3. Roll up from the longest edge to form a neat roll. Repeat with remaining pastry and filling.

4. Cut each roll into 5cm (2in) lengths, pinch edges together and roll into neat balls.

5. Deep-fry balls in hot oil until golden brown and filling is cooked through, about three minutes. Serve hot. Makes approximately 16.

Stuffed Chicken Wings

The decor of The New Dynasty Restaurant, Cremorne, Sydney, is one of the most attractive in town. The menu is wide and varied, the food is delicious. We particularly liked this succulent way with chicken wings.

YOU WILL NEED:
12 chicken wings
1 slice ham
1 bamboo shoot
2 dried mushrooms
3 shallots
1 egg-white

SAUCE:
4 teaspoons tomato sauce
2 teaspoons sugar
2 teaspoons soy sauce
1 teaspoon worcestershire sauce
¼ cup water

SAUCE:
Place all ingredients into pan, stir until boiling.

1. Cut chicken tip and small drumstick off each chicken wing, leaving one thick piece from each wing. (Cut-off pieces can be used for chicken stock, soup etc.)

2. Drop chicken wings into boiling salted water, cook for five minutes, drain, allow to cool. Make two light cuts on the underside of each wing at both ends. Loosen meat away from bone with small sharp knife. With a twisting movement remove bones.

3. Cover mushrooms with water, leave for 30 minutes, drain, squeeze dry. Cut bamboo shoot into 1cm (½in) slices, then cut into 5mm (¼in) strips. Cut shallots, mushrooms and

ham into strips about the same size. Insert one stick of each ingredient into the hole left by the bone; trim ends neatly.

4. Dip chicken wings into lightly beaten egg-white, deep-fry in hot oil until golden brown. Drain on absorbent paper. Put on serving plate, pour sauce over.

Honey Prawns

The Dragon City Restaurant, in the Old Windsor Tavern, corner of Castlereagh and Park Streets, Sydney, is a fairly new restaurant that is fast becoming popular, not only for its convenient mid-city location, but for the quality of its food. Honey Prawns is one of their specialities.

YOU WILL NEED:
750g (1½lb) green king prawns
cornflour
1 cup self-raising flour
½ teaspoon salt
pinch pepper
1¼ cups water
1 egg
oil for deep-frying
1 tablespoon oil, extra
2 tablespoons honey
sesame seeds

1. Shell prawns, make a slit down back of each prawn, remove back vein. Coat prawns in cornflour. Shake off excess.

2. Sift flour, salt and pepper into a bowl. Make a well in the centre. Gradually add combined water and beaten egg. Mix to a thin batter, beat until smooth and free of lumps. Put three or four prawns in a small bowl, pour a small amount of batter over them, mix with a fork, to coat prawns. Repeat with remaining prawns.

3. Heat oil in large pan or wok, add prawns, a few at a time. Cook for a few minutes until prawns are golden and cooked through. Remove all oil from pan, wipe clean.

4. Heat extra oil in pan, add honey, stir over gentle heat until mixture is heated through. Add prawns, toss in honey mixture to coat prawns; remove from pan, sprinkle with sesame seeds. Serves 4.

Pork Chops with Plum Sauce

There are many Chinese restaurants in Sydney's Eastern suburbs; the Rose Bay Chinese Restaurant is one of the most popular. The following recipe is a favourite at this restaurant.

YOU WILL NEED:
6 pork leg chops
3 teaspoons cornflour
2 tablespoons dry sherry
1 tablespoon soy sauce
1 tablespoon hoi sin sauce
1 teaspoon sesame oil
1 teaspoon sugar
½ teaspoon salt
½ cup water
¾ cup bottled plum sauce
2 dried red chillies
2 tablespoons oil

1. Remove rind and surplus fat from chops, cut chops into large strips. Put into bowl with combined cornflour, dry sherry, soy sauce, hoi sin sauce, sesame oil, sugar and salt. Leave to stand one hour.

2. Drain pork, reserve marinade. Heat oil in pan or wok, add pork, toss until golden brown, about 10 minutes.

3. Put water, plum sauce, finely chopped red chillies and reserved marinade in saucepan. Stir until combined. Stir until boiling, remove from heat.

4. Add prepared sauce to wok, stir until sauce boils and thickens. Reduce heat, simmer, covered 15 minutes. Serves 6.

Chicken Hotpot

The Eastern Restaurant, Dixon Street, Sydney, has all the popular Chinese dishes — as well as some simple, delicious examples of Chinese home-style cooking — such as this recipe for Chicken Hotpot. We've cooked the whole recipe in one pot, but the Eastern cooks in small, individual pots.

YOU WILL NEED:
1.5kg (3lb) chicken
cornflour
30g (1oz) dried mushrooms
5 slices green ginger
4 shallots
¼ cup oil
1 clove garlic
2 teaspoons cornflour, extra
¼ cup chicken stock
½ cup dry white wine
1 tablespoon soy sauce
½ cup chicken stock, extra

1. Put mushrooms in bowl, cover with hot water, let stand 30 minutes, drain, squeeze dry. Joint chicken, cut into small serving-size pieces, coat well with cornflour. Cut shallots into 5cm (2in) lengths.

2. Heat oil in pan or wok, add half the chicken pieces, cook until golden brown,

remove from pan, repeat with remaining chicken. Return all chicken to pan.

3. Add mushrooms, shallots, sliced ginger and crushed garlic to pan, toss one minute. Add combined extra cornflour, chicken stock, white wine and soy sauce. Stir until sauce boils and thickens.

4. Put chicken into hotpot, add extra chicken stock, cover. Bake in moderate oven approximately 25 minutes or until chicken is tender. Serves 6.

Toffee Apples

Toffee Apples are a favourite Chinese dessert. Few restaurants make them better than the Peking Palace, Cremorne, Sydney. The Peking Palace has many unusual items on its menu, including Szechuan food.
A wok is necessary when making the toffee for this dessert; a saucepan would not be able to generate the necessary high, wide-spread heat.

YOU WILL NEED:
2 medium-size green apples
1 cup plain flour
1 cup water
2 teaspoons oil
oil for deep frying

TOFFEE:
2 teaspoons oil
2 cups sugar
1 cup water
2 tablespoons sesame seeds

1. Peel apples, cut into quarters, remove cores. Cut each quarter in half across to form 16 pieces.

2. To make the batter sift flour into bowl, add oil and water gradually. Stir until smooth. Drop apple pieces into batter, drain off excess batter, then deep fry in hot oil until light brown. Drain on absorbent paper.

3. To make the toffee heat oil in wok, add water and sugar, stir until boiling. Increase heat to highest,

continue stirring rapidly. A wide metal draining spoon rather than a wooden spoon is best for this. After about five minutes' rapid stirring, mixture will go white and foamy, almost as if sugar has crystallized. Continue to stir rapidly another five minutes and toffee will become clear. Continue to stir another two to three minutes until toffee turns a light golden colour.

4. Remove from heat immediately, add sesame seeds and apples, toss lightly. Turn out immediately onto plate which has been well greased with sesame oil.

5. Using chopsticks, pick up toffee-coated apple, put into bowl filled with iced water and ice cubes. Have lots of ice cubes in the iced water otherwise the hot toffee will soon warm the water.

126

Index

Opposite page: Melon
with Champagne, page 100.